# ELSE VON DER TANNE

# ELSE VON DER TANNE

by WILHELM RAABE

*with Translation and Commentary
and an Introduction to Raabe's Life and Work*

by

James C. O'Flaherty and Janet K. King

THE UNIVERSITY OF ALABAMA PRESS

*University, Alabama*

# *Preface*

The recent striking revival of interest in the works of Wilhelm Raabe (1831–1910) has been accompanied by a thoroughgoing reappraisal of his entire authorship. One of the earlier Novellen, *Else von der Tanne*, has become the subject of considerable interest in the past few years. Not that earlier critics did not recognize its merits. Far from it. But the special attention given to this particular work is due to a growing awareness of its relevance to the human situation—particularly that of twentieth century man —and further to an increasing sensitivity to the unusual artistry of this finely wrought Novelle. Regarding the first point, a German critic wrote shortly after the Second World War:

> [*Else von der Tanne*] is no longer a story that happened at some remote time in the past. It is a thing of our own flesh and blood, of our own heart and soul. We can testify to the effect that it is an event which deeply concerns us and which carries a solemn warning for the days to come. Never before in our lives have we been so open to the reception of *Else von der Tanne*.[1]

In addition to its contemporaneity and its immediate appeal when simply read for the moving narrative, the Novelle challenges the thoughtful reader by confronting him with several levels of meaning at once. Biblical interpreters of an earlier day were accustomed to speak of the fourfold sense of Scripture. In a somewhat similar vein we may speak of the threefold sense of Raabe's *Else von der Tanne*, for it challenges us on the levels of aesthetic, moral, and religious meaning. But it is a challenge which is not so easily met if one approaches the work without any assistance. In a recent study Stanley Radcliffe remarks that Raabe's work "always demands a careful reading," maintaining that *Else* is no exception.[2] Therefore, the Introduction and rather full

v

Translator's Notes are designed to provide the reader with the necessary aids to interpretation.

The German text reproduced in the following pages is that of *Wilhelm Raabe. Sämtliche Werke,* eds. Karl Hoppe, Hans Oppermann, and Hans Plischke, Braunschweiger Ausgabe (Göttingen, 1962), IX, part 1, pp. 159–198.

## Notes

1. Alfred Ehrentreich, "Else von der Tanne," *Die neue Schau,* X, Kassell, 1949, 300.

2. "Wilhelm Raabe, The Thirty Years War, and the Novelle," *German Life and Letters* XXII, 3 (April, 1969), 228.

## *Acknowledgments*

I wish to express my appreciation to the following persons who have been especially helpful in the preparation of the work: the late Professor Samuel J. Pease of the German Department of the University of Kansas, Pittsburgh, Kansas, who years ago encouraged me to render the Novelle into English in the first place; Professors Ralph S. Fraser and Wilmer D. Sanders of the German Department and Professor Robert N. Shorter of the English Department of Wake Forest University; Professor Janet K. King, University of Texas, all of whom read the translation with a critical eye and whose recommendations were most helpful. Above all I would like to thank my wife, Lucy R. O'Flaherty, who aided me in countless ways with the project from the beginning and whose hand is most evident in the translation of the two poems in the text. I am deeply grateful to the Research and Publication Fund of Wake Forest University and the Piedmont University Center for their generous support of publication.

J.C.O'F.

My thanks to Professor Walter Wetzels of the Department of Germanic Languages, University of Texas at Austin, for sharing his mind and his time with characteristic generosity. His insights and enthusiasm are reflected in these pages. To Professor James C. O'Flaherty of the German Department of Wake Forest University, my gratitude for enlisting me in this joint venture and assisting me in every possible way.

J.K.K.

# CONTENTS

# Introduction

From the outset, one of the most striking features of Wilhelm Raabe's life is its apparent inconsistency. A most congenial man, his regular *Stammtisch* visits with friends and acquaintances in Braunschweig were concurrent with the appearance of novels which presented a critical view of the very petty bourgeoisie with whom he enjoyed associating. A man widely read in philosophy as well as ancient and modern literatures, Raabe was loath to credit even latent influences upon his writing. He kept a diary which bore virtually uninterrupted daily notations from October 1, 1857 to November 2, 1910, yet avoided recording all but the most enigmatic references to personal feelings. Diary remarks concerning depression or anxiety contain absolutely no explanation or hint as to their origin. Raabe is thought of as an extremely reticent author. He resented a great deal of what was written about him and actually undertook to suppress some publications such as Herman Krüger's *Der junge Raabe* (*The Young Raabe*, [1911]), which appeared posthumously in Krüger's deference to the author's wishes. On the other hand Raabe encouraged to the extent of a lively correspondence with Wilhelm Kosch a university seminar devoted to his work.

Such seeming contradictions between the author's public and private image were to have unfortunate results for both scholarly and public reception of Raabe. Shortly after his death a small circle of devoted admirers formed a "Raabe Society" (Raabegesellschaft) ostensibly to expand the author's reading public. In actuality the members' nationalistic fervor and dedication to their mentor as an apostle of "Germanic identity" led to a posthumous body of criticism and popular attitudes which would most surely have been abhorrent to him. Certainly the resulting conception that the author's work should be read in terms of his life and per-

1

sonal ethics is clearly refuted in Raabe's own statements on the subject: "In regard to biographical data, the encyclopedia will have to suffice. I have never experienced anything which could be of the slightest interest to anyone," he assured the *Society for the Advancement of the Arts* at the age of seventy.[1] Efforts to shift public interest from himself to his work were largely unsuccessful. The limited audience Raabe has enjoyed until very recently is due in no small portion to the critical and popular focus on nationalistic and ethical rather than aesthetic and literary implications of his writing. The objective of the remarks which follow is to present facts and to clarify possible misconceptions about the author which have, in the past, interfered with appreciation of his artistic merits.

In 1861, two years before commencing work on the Novelle *Else von der Tanne*, Raabe was asked by a contemporary for biographical data. At the time Raabe was living with his mother in Wolfenbüttel. He had recently returned from Berlin, where he had written a modestly successful novel and was recognized as a promising young author. He was twenty-nine years old. Within twelve months Raabe was to marry and move to Stuttgart for an eight-year interval during which *Else* and three of his best known novels, *Hungerpastor* (1863), *Abu Telfan* (1867), and *Der Schüdderump* (1869) were to be written. The remarks, written originally as letters, provide a starting point for examining the anomalies of Raabe's personality. They also represent comments from a period in his life which is notably lacking in first-hand observations. Translated excerpts from these statements read as follows:

> I was born on the 8th of September in 1831 at Eschershausen in the Weser area of Braunschweig. I received my initial education in the elementary schools and college preparatory school at Holzminden and Oldendorf, the latter community being the location where my father died in 1845 while local justice of the peace. At the preparatory school in Wolfenbüttel I learned little more than drawing and writing German. In 1849 I was sent to Magdeburg

to learn the bookseller's trade. The attempted effort resulted in total failure and would have been ruinous for me if I hadn't boldly extricated myself. I returned home a sick man, but threw myself into a resumed education with great enthusiasm. By 1854 I was ready to attend the University of Berlin where I remained until 1856. My brain had managed to assimilate a considerable amount of fairly confused information which I was now ready to clarify and put in order. I proceeded to do so to the extent of my capabilities. Without friends or acquaintances in the city I was left to my own devices and created a little private world amid the turmoil. In the summer of 1855 I wrote my *Chronik der Sperlingsgasse* which appeared in print in 1857. One might designate this work as a pathological peculiarity. . . .

Subject to inertia and indolent to a very high degree, I am nonetheless capable of enormous industry. I seldom give up a goal, plan, or wish. I tenaciously cling to my original ideas although years may have intervened since their inception. I have never been able to read my way through a French classic tragedy. My understanding of and interest in antiquity is quite limited. I just started reading Goethe three years ago. I still haven't finished *Wilhelm Meister*. On the other hand I had already learned *Faust I* by heart while in Magdeburg. I have read less Jean Paul than one might think. Of his works I own only the two first parts of *Siebenkäs* and *Katzenberger*. Fragments of Schiller have, when read in the right frame of mind, made a considerable impression on me. I am full of contradictions and since earliest childhood I have tortured myself analyzing them. In social life no one would recognize the poet in me. A conversation with aesthetic overtones can drive me to despondency. Because I am by nature somewhat dull and shy, people frequently consider me arrogant and presumptuous. Be that as it may, why continue to describe to you my irridescent soul? I'm quite certain you have had enough and more than enough as it is. . . .[2]

The laconic tone of these apparently matter-of-fact statements is deceptive. A number of facts, when weighed against Raabe's presentation of events, reveal that the author chose to delete or gloss over relevant experiences. For example, Raabe does not mention that the sudden death of Gustav Raabe in 1845 left his mother and her three children virtually penniless and that the father's absence was keenly felt. Some reflection of the impact of this event is witnessed in the recurring figure of the orphan or the child with only one parent throughout Raabe's writing. The specific effect of this loss upon Raabe himself is attested by the author later in life. He described his father as a man of very strong will whose death was a turning point in the poet's life. Had his father lived, Raabe felt that he would probably have been constrained to graduate and continue university studies along traditional lines, probably becoming a lawyer like his father (*Raabe—Gedenkbuch*, Constantin Bauer and Hans Martin Schulz, ed. [1921], p. 8).

Raabe gave no hint in his comments to Thaddäus Lau that the move to Wolfenbüttel was made in part with his own schooling in mind. One of his mother's brothers was a teacher, another the director of the Wolfenbüttel Gymnasium. School essays from this period reveal a thinly disguised resentment toward the constrictions and authoritarian character of the educational system. Whether for these or other reasons, Raabe did not do satisfactory schoolwork. When he left Wolfenbüttel in 1849 it was without the *Abitur*, a prerequisite in Germany for admission to formal university training.

Since Raabe's interests seemed to be in "drawing and writing," the decision to become a bookseller appears natural. Why his attempts to learn this trade resulted in "total failure" and were nearly ruinous for Raabe remains unclear. Virtually all correspondence from this period has been lost and Raabe was, here as elsewhere, reluctant to go into details. The impression left by the autobiographical sketch of 1861 that this time was utterly wasted is incorrect. During the four years spent with the Creutz bookstore in Magdeburg, Raabe read voraciously and laid the foundation for a literary breadth which included French and English as well as German authors. Concerning his reading habits he wrote Wilhelm Kosch almost forty years later: "I read everything which fell into my hands—W. Scott, Dumas the elder, and that which was available in German during the Thirties—Hauff, E. T. A. Hoffmann, etc. Just everything! English authors too, of course, but it was only in Magdeburg that I really developed an interest in them, especially in Thackeray. For his sake I learned English while there and *Pendennis* is the only book of that kind which I actually purchased. The young potential author of the story intrigued me even then." [3]

Raabe also omits mention of the fact that he returned to Wolfenbüttel in 1853 not only to "clarify" his thinking, but to resume his efforts toward an *Abitur* as well. He was twenty-two at this time and his tenacious adherence to once conceived goals attested in the autobiographical remarks must have been sorely put to the test. This second attempt also ended in failure and thus Raabe's Berlin studies could not be undertaken with a view toward eventual graduation. Moreover, he was beginning his university work at an age when normally students were obtaining their degrees. Small wonder then that he found himself isolated and developed little contact with fellow students. Raabe was later to develop parallels to this experience in one of the major themes in his writing: the position of the outsider, the alienated or rejected individual whose achievements and *Weltanschauung* were based on personal standards rather than those of society.

Despite loneliness, Raabe's situation in Berlin was not completely disadvantageous. Since there was no necessity for a specific course of study towards a degree, he was free to attend classes according to his inclinations. Enrolled for a total of four semesters from the summer of 1854 through the winter semester of 1856, Raabe heard lectures on history ranging from Spanish and Arabic cultural backgrounds to Albrecht Dürer's life and work. In philosophy he studied under disciples of Hegel and in the field of literature he attended lectures on Shakespeare's dramas, the history of German literature after Schiller, Goethe, and the *Nibelungenlied*.

Raabe's notebooks written in conjunction with these courses

lie in the city archives in Braunschweig. Although the Germanist
Karl Hoppe has published excerpts from these lecture notes, no
larger study has been made of the extent to which the university
influenced Raabe's personal and creative point of view. Certainly
the frequent allusions in his novels and shorter works to manifold
facets of art, literature, and philosophy can be at least in part at-
tributed to knowledge gleaned in this period. A lifelong pref-
erence for historical and quasi-historical subject matter may also
have received significant impetus at this time. The following
translation from excerpts of Raabe's notes gives some indication
of what these directions may have been:

> What depth Mozart infused into the trivial text of the Magic
> Flute! A poet, grasping an historical subject which has not been,
> up to that time, comprehended, rendered meaningful. Shakespeare
> composing his dramas on the basis of Italian Novellen, old ballads
> (Lear) and sagas—how much difference in his depiction of the
> themes, exploring their depths. The poet who cannot penetrate
> [such events] at greater depth is a mere imitator. Only the in-
> ventive faculty can recreate an epoch.[4]

No scholar has better expressed the trademark of Raabe's historical perspective: human experience so depicted as to animate
dates and place names in an entirely new chronography.
     The value of the preparation which Raabe received is at least
partially reflected in his initial literary undertaking, *Die Chronik
der Sperlingsgasse*. Although it may have appeared to its author
in 1861 a "pathological peculiarity," it proved to be one of
Raabe's most widely read novels and is considered by some
scholars today to be "as expertly written as any of his books"
(Barker Fairley, *Wilhelm Raabe* [1961], p. 188). The discursive
description of the inhabitants of the "Sparrow Street" is inter-
spersed with diary notations, letters, and ruminations of the
lonely and elderly narrator, Johannes Wacholder. The actual
chronological events in the novel are subordinated to Wacholder's memories. Present happenings unfold in terms of a panorama

of antecedents; Raabe is concerned to fit the past into a meaningful juxtaposition with the present.

The initial public and critical response to *Die Chronik* was heartening if hardly overwhelming. Thus Lau was interested in printing autobiographical material about Raabe largely on the basis of this work which the author refers to with such deprecation. What he reveals about himself is little more than the fact that he is a promising young writer, circumspect about personal matters, reluctant even in 1861 to discuss more than the framework of events which formed his experience heretofore. In certain respects this picture changed as Raabe matured. In appraising his writing, he was to become more objective and articulate. Indeed, during an era of positivism in literary criticism when a man's biography was equated with his literature as a matter of course, Raabe was an outspoken critic of such methods applied to his writing. He consistently advocated examining formal qualities of his work rather than seeking in them ethical models or a philosophy of life.

Nor were these views the defense of a withdrawn personality as the self-appraisal of 1861 might imply. The charge of provincialism frequently leveled at Raabe has only qualified justification. True, the author removed himself from contact with the power structure of the socalled "Founder's Period" (*Gründerzeit*) which followed German unification in 1871. On the other hand the relocation from Wolfenbüttel to Stuttgart in 1862 brought Raabe into a kind of cultural center from whose vantage point he was to associate not only with contemporary writers and publishers, but with continuing political activity as well.

The move, coinciding as it did with Raabe's marriage to Bertha Leiste, indicates that the author was making a conscious effort to expose himself to a more cosmopolitan atmosphere. In Berlin Raabe had been "without friends and acquaintances." During the eight year sojourn in Stuttgart, he established relationships which were to last a lifetime. Several friendships stemmed from involvement in the newly founded German Party (*Deutscher National-*

*verein*). The intention of the party had been to combat separatist groups and work for a unified Germany, an issue which was clouded by the war between Prussia and Austria in 1866. In pro-Austrian Swabia, Raabe's unconcealed conviction that national unity should stem from Prussia rather than the Hapsburg empire resulted in his expulsion, along with others of this sympathy, from the Stuttgart branch of the "German Party" in 1866. Concerning the political and social climate of the community at this time, Raabe wrote his mother that he was beginning to find distasteful the "particularist narrow-mindedness" predominating in Stuttgart (5.16.1866).

Although the war was soon over, Raabe felt a continuing breach in its aftermath. Consideration of a move from Stuttgart is noted in his diary as early as 1865 and there is little doubt that political as well as personal developments helped prompt the entry of September 28, 1868, which reads simply "Decision to move to Braunschweig." Why Raabe tarried until 1870 is not clear. Hermann Pongs suggests the mobilization of Prussian troups overcame his reluctance to leave. On the basis of letters written shortly before Raabe's death, Pongs views the move as reflective of a "loss of equilibrium," a period of intense loneliness with resultant negative effects upon the author's writing style (*Raabe*, [1958], p. 297). Karl Hoppe disputes Pong's assumption, arguing that Raabe's diary notations concerning a warm welcome in Braunschweig by friends and relatives hardly reflect social alienation. Hoppe suggests it is more accurate to speak of a strictly literary isolation which was already amply evident to the author during the later Stuttgart years. Indicative of discouragement is a letter of July 3, 1869 in which Raabe writes his mother: "I find the 'broader reading public' ignores me more and more." [5] This state of affairs is expressed even more emphatically in a letter written by Bertha Raabe to a friend shortly after the impending departure had been formally announced. "To be sure there is nothing new to write about in Stuttgart. New to me, however, is that one must say goodbye to a city to be appreciated by the people who live here . . . Hallberger [a publisher] rejected the *Schüd-derump* manuscript with the warmest regards, and now he wants to build him [Raabe] a house, if only he will stay." [6] Hence the move to Braunschweig is probably most accurately described as recognition of an existing situation rather than precipitation of it. Raabe must have seen little point in remaining in a cultural center where he was largely ignored. Historical events had revealed that Stuttgart had its share of intransigence. At least in Braunschweig the local provincialism would be in sympathy with the author's own political convictions.

Notwithstanding the lack of contact in regard to both literary and political developments after 1870, Raabe found no dearth of social connections in Braunschweig. Membership in a variety of clubs and local civic efforts provided ample associations. Herman Helmers explains the apparent contradiction of the anti-bourgeois Raabe placing himself in the center of middle class undertakings as simply the only recourse available to a man who enjoyed the company of other people (*Wilhelm Raabe*, [1968], p. 8). Surely it is understandable that an author whose life work went largely unappreciated had a desire for the kind of personal admiration he received from friends like the Gymnasium teacher Wilhelm Brandes and the circle of visitors who came to seek Raabe out in "Herbsts Weinstuben" in later years.

In recent criticism there has been a growing tendency to attribute to the Braunschweig period Raabe's best and most characteristic work. Raabe's own comments imply that he came to see his efforts more and more in terms of "early" and "late" Raabe. "In Berlin . . . [my] admirers have taken into account only the first twenty years . . . The following twenty-five, in my opinion the first truly fruitful years, are not considered." [7] The author delineates the period even more sharply the following month in a letter to Siegmund Schott. "They are writing 'words of wisdom' about Raabe already? Oh, if only people had wanted to look for it a bit more over the past fifteen years!" [8] And in 1905 weighing the relative merits of *Schüdderump* (1870) and *Stopfkuchen*

(1890), he found the former "certainly a good book, but it was with *Stopfkuchen* that I found myself freest and most confident. . . ." [9]

One basis for dating this distinction of "early" and "late" Raabe at about 1870 is the predominance of shorter works prior to that time. Only eleven of Raabe's twenty-nine completed novels had been written by 1870 as opposed to twenty-five of the thirty-eight works designated by Raabe as either "narratives" or "Novellen." After the move to Braunschweig, longer works predominate whose epic breadth allows greater development of Raabe's characteristic themes and stylistic techniques.

The predominant theme throughout Raabe's writing was already evident in *Die Chronik:* the development of the individual exposed to historical and contemporary events largely beyond his control. Raabe is a master at depicting the implications of this conflict within a middle-class milieu. Other social spheres were simply less familiar to the author; when he dwells on the proletariat, the rural peasantry, or refers to the social elite and the nobility, Raabe does not develop his characters beyond vague generalizations. The role of the villagers in *Else von der Tanne* as an anonymous group characterized largely by allusions to vindictive, barbaric behavior illustrates this trait. Similarly, criticism of upper classes such as that found in *Hungerpastor* or *Abu Telfan* tends to be couched in middle-class preconceptions about the moral turpitude of the affluent rather than practical political and social issues. In this sense, as he was probably aware, comparisons with Dickens and Thackeray put the author at a disadvantage. Raabe presented neither widespread social abuses nor the broader spectrum of society convincingly, and attempts to do so fall largely in the period before 1870. After the retreat to Braunschweig he concentrated in the main on the pastors, doctors, students, teachers, and tradesmen he could draw so perceptively. Along with this greater concentration upon a middle-class setting, a new narrative point of view was to develop.

The individuals around whom Raabe's early narratives center are, generally by reason of birth or circumstances, outsiders. Hans

Unwirsch (*Hungerpastor*) literally hungers for knowledge about life and a meaningful existence, but his search is largely as an onlooker rather than a participant in events. He discovers good and bad models of behavior from which he learns without actually involving himself to the extent of changing or developing his personality. In *Abu Telfan* the central figure is Leonhard Hagebucher, who returns to Europe after a period of captivity in Africa only to feel as much a prisoner in Nippenburg, the town which had once been his home. Initially Raabe levels strong criticism at the petty provincialism viewed by Hagebucher and like-minded friends. By the close of the novel, however, a resigned reconciliation has taken place. Thus a work which commences as an attack on bourgeois values is resolved in a weak, unsatisfying fashion. Apparently Raabe was himself unable at this point to reconcile favorable with unfavorable aspects of what he termed "German philistinism."

*Schüdderump*, more than any other single work, is responsible for the erroneous popular notion that Raabe was a pessimistic author with a negative view of life. The external events lend themselves to this interpretation. The child Toni Häussler is brought to the poorhouse in a small community by means of a *Schüdderump* or death cart, the latter recurring again periodically throughout the novel. Toni is rescued after her mother's death by the local gentry, the von Lauens, and raised as a member of the family. As she approaches young womanhood her disreputable grandfather decides to exploit the girl and, largely through factors beyond his or Toni's control, succeeds in taking her away to Vienna. She dies there, the representatives from the von Lauen household arriving too late to save her.

In these, as well as other works of the earlier period, a strong thread of passivity emerges. The major figures, whether men or women, are pawns of fortune, their efforts at self-assertion brief and unfruitful. Frequently, as in the case of Toni and many young heroines of early narratives—Else among them—the chief characters are most accurately described as victims of events. They are exposed to problems which may educate, reconcile, strengthen or even kill them, but basically they cannot alter events or resolve their individual conflicts. In this sense character development in the works prior to 1870 was largely the province of accident.

With the Braunschweig period the central figures change. The garrulous narrator of *Die Chronik* reappears more frequently and his functions are elaborated upon. One can more accurately speak of the narrators, for these later works often have multiple story-tellers with the first-person narrator secondary to the one or more third-person versions which he relates. No longer complete outsiders, these people function more or less comfortably within the middle-class milieu. No longer entirely passive, they depict themselves in a struggle to come to grips with philistinism on their own terms. They emerge with a personal system of values and convictions intact.

In *Stopfkuchen*, like *Abu Telfan*, the narrator returns from Africa. Eduard, like Leonhard Hagebucher, comes back to his insular childhood home. Unlike Leonhard, Eduard does discover someone in this environment who has accepted what he found worthwhile and has maintained the integrity of the objective observer. In this capacity, Heinrich Schaumann, Eduard's childhood acquaintance, has developed insights about life which are broader than those of the world traveler, and it is Schaumann's story which forms the bulk of the novel. Although he has remained at home, Schaumann has dealt with virtually all the problems of man. Physical confinement has not set spiritual or intellectual limitations upon this unusual individual. Rejecting conventional attitudes, Schaumann has managed to create a personal oasis through perception and tolerance. Despite his wider range of experience, Eduard recognizes that his friend's knowledge and intuitions about human behavior exceed his by far. This positive depiction of an individual drawing the best from the provincial setting and finding it a fruitful, if often painful, training ground where the responsive could learn to cope with all facets of life is representative of Raabe's character delineations in works written after 1870.

In *Stopfkuchen,* as elsewhere in his mature writing, Raabe no longer attempts to deal with social or political complexities except on the fringes of his narratives or as agents responsible for basic human problems, such as a man relinquishing his family heritage in the face of industrial progress (*Pfisters Mühle* [1884]). Therefore the reader who looks for social perspectives in these later novels will be disappointed. But if he is seeking finely individualized portrayals of feeling and aware human beings facing the minor, often absurd and humorous dilemmas which are timeless regardless of social or historical background, there are few authors who do this with greater sensitivity than Wilhelm Raabe.

The author's last completed novel was *Hastenbeck* (1898), and although he worked on a fragment, *Altershausen,* until 1902, it was apparent that he felt his work was completed. Friends' and admirers' urgings that he continue writing were gently repulsed: "I've hung my poeticizing on the wall at the age of seventy. For it is better that people say 'Too bad he has stopped' than that they growl 'Really, he could quit anytime now. . . .' " [10] Despite the fact that he was receiving awards and recognition during the last decades of his lifetime, it remained clear to Raabe that his late work, his most significant work, had gone unnoticed: "The public seems completely satisfied with the youthful nonsense I have long since disregarded, *Chronik* and *Hungerpastor,* and leaves me sitting with all the rest of it." [11] Several months before his death he responded to a publisher's request that the fragment *Altershausen* be completed saying, "Tying together the loose ends of *Altershausen* for your purposes simply cannot be done. It is a bitter thing that I began in the years 1899 and 1900 to fabricate basically for me and me alone. . . ." [12] Raabe died on November 15, 1910, the date when he had commenced writing fifty-six years earlier.

*Else von der Tanne* can be read for enjoyment without reference to extensive commentary. The work possesses the timeless quality of its theme: the extinction of inviolate purity in a carnal world. The historical setting lends itself to ahistorical comparisons, since a society is depicted which has been ravaged morally and physically by the Thirty Years War. The effects of war's devastation provide the background and atmosphere of the narrative. Analogies to more recent catastrophes have prompted commentaries such as Alfred Ehrentreich's "Else von der Tanne—A Refugee's Plight" (*Die neue Schau*, X [1949], 300).

The very fact that *Else* can be read by today's reader in terms of our times may be misleading, however. In equating a literary work with personal experience, formal aesthetic features which are integral to a writer's intentions can easily be overlooked. To appreciate the implications embedded in Raabe's stylistic complexities, the reader must have not only awareness of detail but a considerable body of background knowledge as well. For precisely this reason, the authors have sought to include biographical information, extensive commentary, and interpretation. In the analysis which follows, I will deal first with the work's structural constituents before discussing a variety of relevant conceptual ramifications.

Initial examination of *Else* will be in terms of its genre, the Novelle. As a literary form the Novelle is not likely to be familiar to the American reader. Shorter prose works written in English are commonly designated short stories. To the German, however, the term Novelle is well known; and, although fine points can be and frequently are debated by scholars, certain characteristics are generally assumed to be present when an author—particularly a 19th century author—makes the claim that his shorter prose work is, indeed, a Novelle.

Inherent to the Novelle is that it must have a central event around which all aspects of the narrative essentially revolve and, unlike the short story which need not show a complete progression of events, the Novelle's conclusion should present a culmination, both of action and the primary considerations upon which these actions were founded. The development of the Novelle is essentially dramatic. One anticipates initial exposition followed by action building toward a climax. The short story, on the other hand, can begin almost anywhere, even at the height of events, and frequently breaks off before a definite conclusion. Hence in the short story the resolution of the plot or implications of events are commonly left to the reader's conjecture. The Novelle, on the other hand, moves toward a kind of prose denouement in which the most effective representatives of this genre tie various narrative threads through explicit or implicit statement. Because the short story is a less prescriptive form and may commence or break off at the author's discretion, scholars refer to its "open" structure. In contrast, the comparatively rigid dictates of the Novelle lend it a more complete or finished appearance described as "closed" form.

The foregoing considerations have been thought so essential that the Novelle's more common structural features are, today, virtually synonymous with this narrative form. A device especially typical for the 19th century Novelle is the "frame" or technique of telling a story within a story. The external tale's relationship to the inner narrative customarily illustrates or states outright the meaning of the inner story's conclusion. The frame usually plays no more than a minor role and may be thought of as a tool which the author employs to lend added perspective and insight to the central or inner tale. The basic circumstances of the Novelle contain a "central event" (*das zentrale Ereignis*). The sequence of incidents with its pattern of rising action has a zenith referred to as the "turning point" (*der Wendepunkt*) in the Novelle which generally coincides with the "central event" around which all other events are focused. Contrary to the usual novelistic procedure, Raabe develops his frame story in *Else* so that it is the equivalent in length and complexity to the inner narrative, thus providing the possibility of a central event in the inner as well as the outer story. A primary theme or "idea" (*die Idee*) is perceived as an essential aspect of the major event or in this instance the two parallel central events. Often this idea finds poetic objectification in a metaphor or central symbol.

The reader will have little difficulty identifying these features in *Else*. The frame is constituted by the pastor's experiences, recounted in the present tense, from twilight until midnight of December 24, 1648. Since the remembered events (or inner story) take a positive course until the stoning of Else, this is clearly the turning point and central event of the inner narrative. Else's actual death, occurring six months later, is the most significant event of the frame story which, in this sense, mirrors the action of the inner tale. Raabe relates both levels—frame and inner story—in terms of an extraordinary tension arising from the parallel structure between his two narrative stages. Thus the implications of Else's stoning (the central event of the inner story) are not fully perceived until Else's death (the core event of the frame).

The fact that a work may contain structural requisites of the genre "Novelle" does not automatically render it a good representative of this form or, for that matter, good reading. Such issues depend upon the execution of the narrative or, to put it another way, the techniques through which the author creates his fictive reality. In *Else* Raabe's craftsmanship is chiefly identifiable in his treatment of three aspects: first, in the focus of events; second, in the narrative point of view; and third, in the realization of the Novelle's idea.

In the first pages, the reader is presented with a mass of information on a variety of seemingly unrelated subjects. The story commences with a weather report describing a raging storm. Next, attention shifts to Pastor Leutenbacher who is laboring over his Christmas sermon. Brief mention of past injuries inflicted by marauding troops, a few remaining books such as the worn Bible, present a desolation relieved only by the large white cat sitting comfortably in a corner by the fire. But the pastor is described as oblivious to his surroundings. Inserted throughout the story between this man's ruminations and expressions of despair is the reiteration of this indifference. In such a context the myriad details concerning past events and present conditions play a kind of counterpoint to the psychological reality of the pastor's state of mind. The effect is that while Leutenbacher is virtually incognizant of his surroundings, we, the readers, are made very much aware of them. The emphasis is clear. The external or frame story stresses Leutenbacher's physical presence while the pastor's conscious self is involved in thought processes rooted in the past, in the remembered story about to unfold. Awareness of the present is related to these memories in subliminal fashion through which the increasing measure of the man's despair is realized in physical suffering as well as conscious grief. Thus the arrival of six year old Else and her father in 1636 presages in the pastor's mind a "so wunderliche Geschichte"; [13] yet, having recalled this much, the pastor ascends into a train of thought which causes him to groan aloud and wring his hands. Later, reflecting on the songs and secrets of the woods Else has taught him, Leutenbacher presses his hands to his face and cries bitterly (178:35—179:1). Midway through the Novelle, after recapitulating in his mind the series of incidents occurring prior to Else's eighteenth birthday when she is stoned by the villagers, the pastor draws three crosses under his sermon. He has completed it in the period between the beginning of the story and the conclusion of the inner narrative's action. Raabe has given no indication that Leutenbacher has done any writing in the interim. In terms of the author's presentation, the sermon is completed without the benefit of the pastor's conscious efforts. The author has stated only that Leutenbacher's thinking is dominated by Else as he works on the Christmas sermon—a sermon to be read to the community responsible for her imminent death. Leutenbacher's labors have been rendered mechanical, not deserving of mention, in contrast to his vivid awareness of Else.

With the mention of the sermon, the return to physical reality is reestablished. The housekeeper brings in the evening meal—a loaf of bread. The cat is seen once more. This respite is brief however. Almost immediately the old crone, Justine, appears at the window begging in exchange for her message that Else must die this night (189:13). The pastor gives her the entire loaf of bread and, oblivious of his housekeeper's concern for his well-being, rushes out into the storm (190:15–19).

Although this resume of the relationship of inner and outer events captures at best only the thrust of the Novelle's rising action, the manner of presentation emerges in a consistent pattern. Until the stoning, Leutenbacher's recall of Else envelops him in spiritual calm. This calm is contrasted with the harsh, unrelenting environment of the frame. Else is not only explicitly the "reinste, heiligste Blume," "die Seele des großen Waldes" (178:32–34), she is implicitly the contrast between material presence and spirituality. The fact that the reader learns of her only through Leutenbacher's memory is a simple but effective means of presenting the spiritual rather than the culpable human figure.

Else is not merely remembered in some objective appraisal but, as the subtitle implies, in terms of the happiness (*das Glück*) she has meant for Leutenbacher. Thus when the inner story is completed, the appearance of Justine has special impact. With Justine's prediction, the author's juxtaposition of idyllic, powerfully vivid remembrances and Leutenbacher's present suffering in a bitterly palpable world comes to an end. The depiction of Else's comforting incorporeal significance to the pastor ceases with the news of her impending death. From this point forward the frame story bears the narrative burden alone. Leutenbacher is left now only with the unbearable present tense. On the first page of the Novelle, earthly life was described as so bitter, "daß man es nur ertragen konnte, indem man es vergaß" (161:15–16). With Else's death, physical existence is unalleviated because it is now devoid of all spiritual refuge. All events focus on this realization.

The technique by which Raabe succeeds in contrasting the spirituality of the inner story with the stark corporeality of the narrative frame draws largely from his subtle transitions in narrative perspective. Essentially the Novelle employs several different, if not always clearly distinguishable, points of view. The first is that of the omniscient author, the detached observer who is in command of all the facts and relates them at his own discretion. Virtually the entire Novelle utilizes this ostensibly noninvolved viewpoint. Therefore the specific occasions are all the more striking when, for a sentence or two, the author does delve into the conscious memory of the pastor and simulate the first person singular.

One such instance is a transition to the frame story which commences with a comment illustrating the technique: "Wollte dieser Schneesturm nimmer zu einem Ende kommen" (178:1)? This exclamation could be made by either Raabe or the pastor. It is followed by a description of the storm in onomatopoetic terms and only at the end of the paragraph is Leutenbacher referred to. The reader is told that through all the turmoil of the elements a song which Else once sang sounds in his ear (178:11–25). Aside from making a deft transition from inner to outer story, the narrator, sharing the consciousness of the storm with Leutenbacher, emphasizes the intensely personal perception of Else which he has. The physical world can be described by the reasonably objective observer. Leutenbacher's relationship with Else is unique and his alone.

The merging consciousness of narrator and Leutenbacher occurs again after Justine's message. "Else, die schöne, junge Else stirbt! Else stirbt! Else stirbt!—" (190:4). The exclamation that Else is dying occurs both prior to this statement and following it. However, in the first instance the subjunctive signaling indirect speech is employed, and in the second case the statement is a direct quotation from Leutenbacher rather than part of the narrative explication. Effectively, the author presents the impact of Else's death as too powerful for him to remain aloof. The narrator allows his consciousness to blend with that of the pastor for a realization which is, in this sense as well, more than Leutenbacher can bear.

This shifting point of view between the frame and the inner story is a more complicated procedure than normally occurs in a Novelle with a frame. The unusual balance between inner and outer has been noted. A further distinction is that the outer story in most Novellen involves persons not directly related to the events of the inner tale. The frame need not be a story at all but rather a situation such as the journey to Canterbury or the *De-cameron*'s nobility fleeing from the plague. External interest can be present—for example, one may be peripherally concerned about whether the storyteller of the *Arabian Nights* will succeed in saving her life—but essentially the tales are begun and concluded within the frame and the outer narrative is of secondary interest. Not so with *Else*. Here, instead of a different set of individuals, the same people are involved on both narrative levels. Moreover, the inner story is not complete in isolation. Else is mortally wounded in the pastor's remembrance, but she does not die at that juncture. The effect of her death upon the pastor is not evident until the scene changes permanently to the frame. The reader may not even be aware of this distinction simply because the context for both narrative levels is the same.

In both, Friedemann Leutenbacher's thought processes, as retold by an omniscient author, are interwoven with a series of events. His thinking determines what will be told. On both levels whether these thoughts are lyrical or despairing, conscious or seemingly involuntary—precisely in the extreme polarity of these recollections—Raabe verges on a stream of consciousness technique. In mixing Leutenbacher's varying levels of awareness in terms of the inner/outer narrative perspective, the author creates an effect which foreshadows 20th century developments in the psychological novel. In the guise of an all-knowing storyteller, Raabe approaches the stream-of-consciousness technique. The author depicts a flow of sensations, thoughts, and associations as though describing both the articulated and the unarticulated cognition of the human mind.

A further narrative consideration is the use of quotations in the story. The quotations which are not cited from actual speech or thought of characters in the Novelle are taken from the Bible. The key citations are from the Old Testament and are thought or uttered primarily by the pastor, particularly at those points in the story when he lapses into deep despondency. At the level of semi-conscious expression, the psychological plausibility of such quotations is evident. They serve a further, possibly for Raabe, more important function: lending Leutenbacher's grief and his character an Old Testament breadth. The frequent occurrence of Biblical language through the frame story raises the tone of the pastor's suffering above the level of mere personal grief. In keeping with this tone the pastor expresses the import of her demise with the archaic, totally encompassing language of a Biblical prophet:

> Jawohl, wehe uns! Es ist geschehen—Gottes Wille ist vollbracht. Er hat seine Hand abgezogen von der Erde, er hat die Völker verstoßen und uns vernichtet; es ist keine Hoffnung und kein Licht mehr in der Welt und wird auch nimmer wieder kommen. . . . Der Herr spottet der Erde, und seinem Lachen lauschet der Antichrist in der Tiefe, stehet und ruft den Seinen: Wacht auf, wacht auf, ihr Fürsten der Nacht!—Der Schein Gottes gehet aus der Welt; stehet zu den Riegeln, ihr Gewaltigen, die Pforten des Abgrundes aufzuwerfen,—unser ist das Reich!" (195:13–30).

By merging the speaking style of the Scriptures with his major characterization at the central event of the Novelle, Raabe has, on a purely linguistic level, elevated Leutenbacher to the stature of a Biblical figure and Else's death to the mythic proportions of a parable of the human condition.

The foregoing discussion of complexities involved in the focus of events and the narrative point of view is inexorably connected to the third consideration to be examined: the realization of the Novelle's idea. Else has emerged from the apparent digressions into a spectrum of past and present reflection as the core around which both inner and outer narrative are crafted. She is the focal point of the hero's conscious and unconscious awareness, a cognizance so powerful that the omniscient narrator approaches identification with Leutenbacher and, on occasion, cannot be distinguished from him at all. Yet important as she is, Else never confronts the reader in the course of lived events. She is remembered by Leutenbacher, and she is remembered in such visionary terms

that the resultant figure is more saintlike than human. The author
enforces this impression with obvious corollaries. Else's birthday
is the nameday of John, the saint who baptized in preparation for
repentance and redemption and foretold the coming of Christ.
After baptism by John, Christ was told by a voice from heaven
that he was the son of God. Both revelation and redemption are
associated with this day in the Christian tradition. This day is also
the summer solstice or longest day of the year and celebrated in
a pre-Christian tradition as the harbinger of life and warmth. Sig-
nificantly Else is stoned on this date, but she does not die until
six months later when the northern hemisphere is shrouded in its
longest night—the winter solstice—and while the Christian world
celebrates the spiritual triumph over darkness in the birth of the
savior, Christ.

Through such legendary prefigurations Else's symbolic role
assumes a supra-Christian, archetypical significance. Her purity
is the goodness of redemption and illumination which is threatened by the forces of evil and darkness. Else's translucent, totally
innocent being which the pastor recalls is not intended to be the
plausible depiction of an actual human, but rather the poetic objectification of the essential idea around which the Novelle re-
volves. Raabe avoids characterizing this idea as the simple dichot-
omy of good and evil through a complex, sometimes seemingly
paradoxical, imagery of light and darkness.

From the beginning of the Novelle Raabe employs allusions to
various kinds of light in a variety of contexts. One context is the
imagery which refers to the villagers. As the pastor stands at his
window brooding over the sermon he must write for the congregation responsible for Else's inevitable death, he is oppressed by
awareness of gathering nightfall. His gloom is only heightened
by the view of two or three lights from the village, because sight
of them causes the pastor to reflect upon the "tierische Verdummung" (163:27) of the human beings cowering about the "matten Flämmchen" (163:28) which their hearths produce. This
illumination offers the pastor neither warmth nor consolation so

that he turns from it, "so wandte sich sein Geist auch von ihnen ab" (163:28). Later, in describing the growing resentment of the villagers toward Else and her father, the gloomy hearths of Wallrode in Elend (171:35) are referred to again.

At the heart of the villagers' superstitious fear of Else's hut in the wood is their opinion that she and her father are sorcerers concerned with "Ungeheuerliches, Furchtbares, Tag- und Licht-cheues" (172:13–14). On the day Else is stoned, they wait for her outside the church "in dem Sonnenschein auf und zwischen den Gräbern" (184:34–35). Raabe states there was not one among them who would not gladly have carried wood with which to burn Else at the stake. They only dare to assault her now in the belief that the girl's magic can be overcome and cast "ins Feuer" (186:8). Here is a light imagery which functions in direct contrast with vital, positive associations. The villager's light is harsh and destructive by day, weak but cunning by night, a luciferous illumination which fosters superstition and ignorance. Theirs is the false light, the destructive flame which lacks the capacity to enlighten.

When Else is first introduced, the light imagery surrounding her has features in common with that of the villagers. She is first described as sitting next to a fire (164:33) and Leutenbacher's initial visit discloses a smoldering fire and the sleeping child who is suddenly awakened by a ray of evening sun which has a "röt-lichen Glanz" (165:28). The eyes of Else's father shine menac-ingly and his glinting raised axe causes the little girl to cry out and cover her eyes (166:18–22). Unambiguous clues to the mystery which surrounds these figures are not provided in such allusions.

The first qualitatively different light images occur when the author commences his description of Else's relationship with Pas-tor Leutenbacher. Part of this difference is attributable to the fact that light and nature symbolism are closely intertwined. Else understands the language of animals, the wind and the light (179: 19–20). She has tamed wild animals. In particular a deer and a dove are her constant companions. Prior to knowing Else, the

pastor had been afraid of the various manifestations of nature—
he was cold in the heat of summer or fearful of his own reflection
in a wooded pool (174:6–7). Else is a revelation of new life for
the pastor (176:10–13) and at her side "schauderte und fröstelte
den Pfarrherrn nicht mehr vor den hohen Geheimnissen der
Natur" (179:17–19). Seeing Else for the second time, he finds the
magic which radiates from her two dark childish eyes (176:3)
totally irresistible. This dark light, characteristic of Else and her
wooded environment, unfolds gradually. Else is compared with
the purest, holiest flower (178:32–33). Her illumination increases
with each succeeding spring and does, in fact, cast a spell over
Leutenbacher, making him young again (179:23–28). Through
Else Leutenbacher is able to perceive the natural world which had
previously been impenetrable and threatening as protective and
the wellspring of life itself. This is Else's sorcery or magic, that
from her emanates the light of physical and spiritual renewal
attested to not only in the Novelle's imagery, but in Else's prox-
imity to references about springtime, greening woods, and blooming flowers as well.

   In events directly preceding and following Else's stoning, the
imagery contrasts the realm which is Else's with that of the villagers in which they believe her to be powerless (185:35—186:9).
Two different spheres of light are established. On the day Else is
stoned, all signs are favorable as long as she and her father remain
in the woods. The summer morning lies pleasant, "lieblich" (181:
25), over the woods and all manifestations of nature respond in
kind. Only when the pair reach the last tree and emerge suddenly
in the bright, "helle" (182:3), sunshine are clear messages given
that they should not continue. The tame deer attempts to halt his
mistress and must be driven away (182:4–10). Justine warns Else
that her shadow precedes her (182:33–35), and the old woman
sings a song of death in living and shadow in sunshine (183:4–7)
which intensifies the foreboding atmosphere now surrounding
Else and her father.

   Justine's oxymorons also point to the logic behind the seeming paradoxes of the light symbolism. The danger to Else comes when she deserts the filtered or secluded light of the woods for the bright light of the open fields outside the village. In the domain where Else is secure and unthreatened, the illumination is muted and is itself green shadow (182:7). Only here can Else's luminance flourish. In both the literal and figurative senses, the harsh, glaring light of the fields and the village conjure up realms where shadows can be cast. Had Raabe relied on psychological motivation to bring Else and her father from their forest refuge, this drastic change in their pattern of living would lack plausibility. Instead the author establishes, through subtle but explicit light imagery, archetypal configurations confronting one another on a level of predestination antedating Christianity.

The final consideration of light symbolism is its relationship to Pastor Leutenbacher in isolation. Here the implications are unambiguous. The entire story transpires between dusk and gradual darkening to midnight. Initially he stands at a window gazing into the darkness and reflecting upon Else. When he learns Else is dying, he rushes out into the snow without hearing his housekeeper, who stands in the hallway with a lamp (190:12), and when he reaches the fields outside the village the wind has swept them clean so that "der kahle schwarze Boden nackt in dem seltsamen Dämmer dalag" (190:21–22). Only when he reaches the high firs near the hut does the storm cease and the pastor glimpses "das ruhige Licht in der Hütte" and at the same time this light seems to recede farther and farther away (192:10–15). His pursuit of the light culminates with the realization that Else is dead; then only does he enter the hut. When he leaves it a few minutes later, the night has become as dark as the terrible night which the pastor has just prophesied in his despair, and the light from the hut has inexplicably disappeared. Leutenbacher's last words are from Lamentations 3:6, a line from the same verses quoted at the outset of the Novelle: "Er hat mich in Finsternis geleget, wie die Toten der Welt" (196:24). The light has been Else and without it the pastor's will to live has been extinguished.

In this sense the Novelle can be said to have two martyrs. Else experiences martyrdom of her physical state but not of the spirit. She, like St. Stephen, the first Christian martyr who also found death by stoning, goes from a state of earthly purity to one of eternal grace. Leutenbacher's martyrdom forms the context of the Novelle. The rebirth of soul which he receives through Else results in an intensity of pain and anguish at her loss which he would otherwise not have known.

In unravelling the threads of a complex, richly woven Novelle, an ultimate question—what did the author intend to say or demonstrate with his story?—inevitably arises. Raabe has explained his images to some extent within the confines of the Novelle. Else is the "soul" of the woods. She is associated with both Christian and natural symbology reflecting life, revelation, and a mysterious "magical" spiritual renewal. Is her death and the death of Leutenbacher a statement of unrelieved pessimism on the part of the author?

The ethical or philosophical overtones in Raabe's writing have led to numerous interpretations and biographical studies attempting to establish particular influences such as Jacob Böhme's mysticism or Schopenhauer's negative views on the results of human endeavor. In point of fact, a diary notation indicates that Raabe purchased a treatise on Schopenhauer just six weeks prior to drawing up his first draft of "Else." Thus it is conceivable that he had some picture of Schopenhauer's major philosophical insights while working on the concept of the Novelle. Comparison of parallels between Schopenhauer's philosophical views and features of Raabe's Novelle does not imply the author was, in fact, illustrating a philosophy or even conscious it existed. Raabe may have developed attitudes similar to but not attributable to Schopenhauer's direct influence. The characteristics which the ideas in a literary work have in common with a philosophical one remain speculation without greater corroboration than exists in this instance. However, the fact that such speculation can be cited reflects both the depth and range of potential within *Else*. At the same time, points of comparison expand the horizon of the Novelle. This is the intent of the brief excursus which follows.

Underlying Schopenhauer's thought is the thesis that the will of all living creatures to continue living is the primary reality of their existence. On the animal level the unconscious will dominates. In the instance of an intelligent being and depending upon the degree of intelligence, the will may manifest itself as conscious desire when the unconscious mechanism has failed to meet the needs of the individual. In any event, the intellect or knowing consciousness is not the primary consideration determining human behavior. The knowing consciousness is subordinate to the desiring consciousness of the will. Furthermore, Schopenhauer believes that life is characterized by unsatisfied wants and recurring pain so that the most indomitable will experiences repeated disappointment. The pain incurred when the will is thwarted may be relieved temporarily by submerging both will and intellect in an overwhelming interest such as science or art. But no matter what the project or how earnest the efforts, the moment of inevitable loss or disillusionment occurs, and the pain of unfulfilled needs, the tyrant will, reasserts itself immediately. In only one exigency can this cycle be checked: by a death to which the will is reconciled. Here lies the virtue of suffering. We are martyred by life for purposes of our deliverance from it. Towards the close of *Die Welt als Wille und Vorstellung*, Schopenhauer sums up the dilemma implicit in the human situation with the following words:

> Truly that which lends our existence its strange and ambivalent character is this—that in that existence two diametrically opposed forces are constantly in conflict: the one, the individual will, oriented toward chimeric happiness in an ephemeral, dreamlike, deceptive existence, where in regard to the past, happiness and unhappiness are a matter of complete indifference (the present, however, becomes the past with every moment); and the other force, the will of destiny, obviously oriented toward the destruction of our happiness and, through it, toward the mortification of our will and the release from the illusions which bind us to the world.[14]

Where are the specific points of similarity between Schopenhauer's view of human aspirations and the depictions in Raabe's Novelle? Schopenhauer views human will as immersed in a futile effort resulting inevitably in "mortification" or self-destruction. To some degree, the capacity for objective assessment of this situation—intellect—can render the mortification of the individual will a release rather than the annihilation of the spirit. Thus Schopenhauer concludes that the human potential for true existence lies in a state of will-lessness, a condition in which both knowing and desiring consciousness are totally suppressed or cease to function. One means of achieving this state is the acceptance of death as a liberation from all desire and hence more real than the phantasmagoria we call life.

Such liberation, either in death or complete subjugation of the will through other means, is possible only to a few since most humans are limited by their inability to perceive or reason out the difference between that which is real and that which is illusory. Concerning them Schopenhauer states: "The weak-minded are not weak merely because they are ignorant and reason incorrectly on occasion. But rather, through the obscurity of their entire thinking process, which is comparable to a bad telescope in which outlines are obfuscated and appear blurred and the various objects run together." [15] The hopelessly insensate human beings the philosopher describes find objectification in Raabe's imagery and direct assessment of the inhabitants of Wallrode in Elend. Repeatedly throughout the Novelle, Raabe demonstrates that Leutenbacher's congregation cannot be reached on the level of reason and fact. For them, events have only irrational explanations based on superstition. Thus the protection against the resentful villagers that Else and her father enjoy is attributable only to the peasants' ignorance, which engenders an aura of what must be shunned and feared about the girl and her father.

Schopenhauer identifies the chief characteristic of inferior intellects as a haziness of their entire thinking process. Raabe indicates a very similar attitude. He too finds the villagers animal-like (163:27) in actual statement, and the author's reluctance to depict individual members of the village with logically or psychologically demonstrable motivation may also be interpreted in this context. Raabe leaves the villagers a vague, anonymous group— as if they were beneath depiction.

If the peasantry is beyond enlightenment, what about the intelligent being who demands more from life than the exercise of the unconscious will? On this level Raabe offers the reader two figures: Pastor Leutenbacher and Else's father, Magister Konradus. The latter figure remains shadowy throughout the Novelle. His tragic personal history is treated as yet another bitter experience which speaks against the possibility for triumph of the individual will. The man has carried on for the sake of his daughter. Unlike Leutenbacher, he has been prepared for the worst and faces his daughter's death as a half-anticipated event. He will continue living in full cognizance that the effort is futile, and it is in this sense that Konradus says to the pastor: "Mein Kind lebt; aber wir die wir Atem holen, wegen unter dem Fuße des Todes" (195:32–33). Konradus' statement repeats the contradiction of life in death foretold in Justine's song. Schopenhauer identifies this paradox as the essential human condition: in order for the individual will to exist, it must participate in life's deception. Renunciation of that deception is the first step in approaching higher reality. Only by eschewing life can this be accomplished. Magister Konradus had done so long before Else's death and hence he can accept that death with a fatalistic equanimity.

The implications of Else's dying are quite different for Pastor Leutenbacher. Prior to knowing Else, the pastor's sole respite from mental and physical suffering had been his school years (162:31–35). Unlike Magister Konradus, Leutenbacher had not suffered the deep personal loss of family, life work, or position in a community. He had lived in a *status quo* of misery in Wallrode. The school years have only a dreamlike quality in his mind, and the author observes that Leutenbacher would have been no better than the lost German people if it had not been for Else von der

Tanne (162:32—163:2). Intellect and education alone would not
have sustained him spiritually for an indefinite period of time.
Raabe's delineation of Leutenbacher's situation is like Schopenhauer's view that the intellect is unable to survive in isolation.
The philosopher does not relegate man's reasoning powers to a
high position because the mind forgets—new ideas and experiences are constantly taking precedence over the old. Schopenhauer envisions only one circumstance under which even the most
steadfast intellect will not falter: only when the cause of the intellect is allied with all components of the will.[16]

Clearly Leutenbacher's feeling for Else represents more than a
sympathy of intellect alone. If the pastor had needed only intellectual companionship, this need would have been met by asso-
ciation with Else's father, a like-minded, highly educated man
with whom Leutenbacher comes to be on close terms (176:16–
28). Raabe indicates in both statements and allusions throughout
the Novelle that Else's significance is qualitatively different from
anyone or anything else. The most frequent comparison, already
discussed in regard to imagery, is that Else is a "soul." Leutenbacher and Else are described as lending objects or situations a
soul. Hence Raabe is not using this term in the connotation of
the immaterial essence belonging to a single human being but
rather as an animating principle which can be transferred to various corporeal entities as well as immaterial concepts. Raabe describes the function of the soul in the following words:

> Aber wenn der Mensch seine Seele gibt, so muß er auch eine Seele
> Wieder empfangen, wenn sich nicht der hohe Segen zum bittersten
> Unheil verkehren soll, und es ist einerlei, ob die Seele einem Weibe,
> einer Dichtung oder einem großen Werk und Plan zum Besten der
> Brüder des Erdentages gegeben werde (173:27–31).

The soul conceived of by Raabe can be contained in a woman,
poetic creativity, or a great project for the betterment of mankind. The specific reference in the Novelle is that the pastor cannot give his soul to the woods unless he receives one in return.

Else lends the woods a soul and is thus compared; or, more accurately, her soul is compared to the essence of "souls" of activities which demand the utmost dedication. Neither artistic endeavor nor humanitarian struggles are characterized by the exercise of intellect in isolation, but rather by the overwhelming aspiration and steadfast inner conviction which involve the total will.[17]

At the outset of the Novelle, Raabe informed the reader that life was made bearable for Friedemann Leutenbacher by his capacity to forget. The impact of the Novelle rests upon the fact that he becomes increasingly unable to dismiss the past, because his very will to live encompasses past, present, and future consciousness of Else. The pastor has no thoughts which do not terminate in considerations of this girl whom the reader comes to know as an ideal potentiality within his mind. From the perspective of Schopenhauerian philosophy, Else can even be viewed as the essence of a visible representation, an ideal within the reality which the philosopher calls the "Ding an sich." Her death is a metaphor of the pastor's renunciation of individual will, the ephemeral deception. In this sense Leutenbacher also experiences life through death. In acceptance of ultimate reality he undergoes a spiritual rebirth. Without realizing what he is doing, the pastor climbs out of the valleys to the highest vantage point in the area, the place from which he had shown Else cities and villages, rivers and streams as they extended into the furthest distance (196:27–31). His last thoughts are that he is already dead and he wonders why he still has consciousness of self under these circumstances. The pastor experiences deliverance through death, and Raabe states simply:

> Else von der Tanne führte die Seele des Predigers aus dem Elend mit sich fort in die ewige Ruhe. Ihnen beiden war das Beste gegeben, was Gott zu geben hatte in dieser Christnacht des Jahres eintausendsechshundertvierzigundacht (197:21–24).

# *Notes*

1. "Für das 'Biographische' müßte unbedingt das Konversationslexicon ausreichen. Ich habe wahrhaftig nichts erlebt, was da die Leute interessieren könnte" (to the *Verein zur Förderung der Kunst, Berlin*, 4.4.1901) *In alls gedultig, Briefe Wilhelm Raabes*, Wilhelm Fehse ed. (Berlin, 1940), p. 346.

2. Ich bin am 8. September 1831 zu Eschershausen im Weserkreis des Herzogthums Braunschweig geboren und erhielt meine erste Erziehung in den Volksschulen und auf dem Gymnasium zu Holzminden und Stadtoldendorf, an welchem letzteren Ort mein Vater 1845 als Justizamtmann starb. Auf dem Gymnasium zu Wolfenbüttel lernte ich wenig mehr als Zeichnen und Deutsch schreiben und wurde 1849 nach Magdeburg geschickt, daselbst den Buchhandel zu lernen. Der Besuch mißlang vollständig und fast wäre ich daran zu Grunde gegangen, wenn ich mich nicht durch einen kühnen Sprung gerettet hätte. Krank kam ich nach Hause zurück, warf mich nun aber mit großem Eifer auf die Studien und konnte 1854 nach Berlin zur Universität gehen, wo ich bis 1856 blieb. Eine ziemliche Menge sehr verworrenen Wissens hatte ich im Hirn zusammengehäuft, jetzt konnte ich Ordnung darein bringen und that es nach Kräften. Ohne Bekannte und Freunde in der großen Stadt war ich vollständig auf mich selbst beschränkt und bildete mir in dem Getümmel eine eigene Welt. Im Sommer 1855 schrieb ich meine *Chronik der Sperlingsgasse*, welche 1857 im Druck erschien. Das Buch ist jedenfalls sozusagen eine pathologische Merkwürdigkeit. . . .

Träge und indolent im höchsten Grade, bin ich doch der größten Energie fähig. Einen Vorsatz, Plan, Wunsch gebe ich selten auf. Ich komme hartnäckig auf den Gedancken zurück, wenn auch Jahre seit dem ersten Auftauchen vergangen sind. Ich habe niemals ein Trauerspiel der französischen Klassiker durchlesen können. Für die antike Welt ist mein Verständniß und meine Theilnahme eine geringe. Goethe lese ich erst seit drei Jahren, den Wilhelm Meister habe ich noch nicht zu Ende gebracht, dagegen wußte ich schon zu Magdeburg den ersten Theil des Faust ganz auswendig. Von Jean Paul habe ich weniger gelesen, als man dencken sollte; ich besitze von ihm nur die beiden ersten Theile des Siebenkäs und den Katzenberger. Schiller macht bruchstückweise und in gewissen Stimmungen großen Eindruck auf mich. Es stecken eine Menge Gegensätze in mir, und seit frühster Jugend habe ich mich selbstquälerisch mit ihrer Analyse beschäftigt. In gesellschaftlichen Leben wird niemand den Poeten in mir erkennen; ein ästhetisches Gespräch kann mich in den Sumpf jagen. . . . Von Natur etwas blöde und scheu, werde ich deßhalb oft für hoffährtig und anmaßend gehalten. Doch was soll ich Ihnen meine schillernde Seele noch weiter schildern. Sie haben gewiß schon genug und übergenug davon . . . (to Thaddäus Lau, 5.23.1861), Fehse, pp. 21-23.

3. "Nachher war mir alles recht, was mir in die Hände fiel, W. Scott, Dumas der Ältere und was im Deutschen in den Dreißigerjahren noch ziemlich neu lag, Hauff, E. Th A. Hoffmann usw.—na, Alles! die englischen Autoren natürlich auch; speziell mit ihnen have ich mich aber erst in Magdeburg beschäftigt, besonders mit Thackeray. Dem zu liebe habe ich dort englisch gelernt und Pendennis ist das einzige Buch der Art gewesen, welches ich mir damals käuflich erwarb. Der junge werdende Autor darin reizte mich eben schon—" (to Wilhelm Kosch, 2.27.1909), Fehse, p. 397.

4. "Was hat Mozart an tiefe aus dem albernen Text der Zauberflöte gemacht! Ein Dichter, das bis dahin noch Ungefaßte, Bedeutende eines historischen Stoffs fassend. Shakespeare, seine Dramen nach italienischen Novellen, alten Balladen (Lear) und Sagen dichtend.—Wie anders stellt er den Stoff dar, seinen tiefern Seiten nach. Wer demgemäß nicht tiefer deuten kann, der ist nur Copist. Epochemachen kann nur der Erfinder—" Karl Hoppe, *Wilhelm Raabe, Beiträge zum Verständnis seiner Person und seines Werkes*, (Gottingen, 1967), p. 18.

5. "Ich finde daß das 'große Publikum' mehr und mehr von mir abwendet." Hoppe, p. 33.

6. "Neues gibt es allerdings nicht in Stuttgart, neu ist mir aber, daß man Stuttgart Lebewohl sagen muß, um bei den Leuten darin Gehebt zu werden . . . Den Schüdderump schickte er [Hallberger] ihm freundlichst grüßend zurück, und jetzt will er ihm extra ein Haus bauen lassen, wenn er bleiben will" (to Maria Jensen, 6.6.1870), Hoppe, p. 31.

7. "Im Berliner Rathhause haben die lieben Gönner nur die ersten zwanzig Jahre meiner litterarischen Laufbahn zu ihrem Feste berücksichtigt: die folgenden fünfundzwanzig, meiner Meinung nach erst wirklich ernteschweren, noch nicht" (to Ferdinand Avenarius, 7.1.1901), Fehse, p. 349.

8. "Sie schreiben schon über Raaben 'Weisheit'? Ja, wenn die Leute nur die letzten 15 Jahre durch ein bißchen mehr in meinen Büchern danach hätten suchen wollen!" (8.4.1901), Fehse, p. 351.

9. "Der *Schüdderump* ist gewiß ein gutes Buch; aber beim *Stopfkuchen* habe ich mich eben am freiesten und sichersten über der Welt empfunden . . ." (to Gotthold Klee, 6.15.1905), Fehse, p. 376.

10. "Was nun uns zwei im besonderen angeht, so kannst Du, auch in Deinen höheren Jahren, in allen Deinen Thatigkeiten weiter wirken; ich dagegen habe mit dem Siebstigsten mein 'Dichten' vollständig an den Nagel gehängt; denn es ist besser, daß die Leute sagen: 'Schade, daß er aufgehört hat!' als daß sie brummen: 'Na endlich konnte er doch aufhören . . .'" (to Karl Schrader, 10.9.1906), Fehse, p. 383.

11. "Da Du Dich auch nach Feder—Neuigkeiten von mir erkundigst,

so sage ich Dir nur: Is nich—Das Volk ist ja völlig befriedigt mit dem
mir abgestandenen Jugendquark: Chronik u Hungerpastor und läßt mich
mit allem Übrigen sitzen" (to Karl Schönhardt, 12.30.1902), Fehse, p. 366.

12. "Die abgerissenen Fäden in 'Altershausen' für Ihren Zweck wieder
an einander zu knüpfen, wird sich nicht machen lassen, es ist ein bitteres
Ding, das ich in den Jahren 1899 und 1900 im Grunde für mich allein zu
spinnen begonnen hatte" (to G. Grotte, 7.13.1910), Fehse, p. 415.

13. Wilhelm Raabe, *Sämtliche Werke*, ed. Karl Hoppe, Hans Oppermann and Hans Plischke (Göttingen, 1962), IX part I, 164:16. Future
references to *Else von der Tanne* are taken from this source and are cited
in the text by page number and line.

14. "Wirklich ist was unserm Leben seinen wunderlichen und zwei-
deutigen Charakter giebt Dieses, daß darin zwei einander diametral ent-
gegengesetzte Grundzwecke sich beständig kreuzen: der des individuellen
Willens, gerichtet auf chimärisches Glück, in einem ephemeren, traum-
artigen, täuschenden Daseyn, wo hinsichtlich des Vergangenen Glück und
Unglück gleichgültig sind, das Gegenwärtige aber jeden Augenblick zum
Vergangenen wird; und der des Schicksals, sichtlich genug gerichtet auf
Zerstörung unsers Glücks und dadurch auf Mortifikation unsers Willens
und Aufhebung des Wahnes, der uns in den Bänden dieser Welt gefesselt
hält." Translated in the text by the author from: Arthur Schopenhauer,
*Sämtliche Werke*, ed. Arthur Hübscher (Wiesbaden, 1949), II, 734–735.

15. "Die schlechten Köpfe sind es nicht bloß dadurch, daß sie schief
sind und mithin falsch urteilen; sondern zunächst durch die Undeutlich-
keit ihres gesammten Denkens, als welches dem Sehen durch ein schlechtes
Fernrohr, in welchem alle Umrisse undeutlich und wie verwischt erscheinen und die verschiedenen Gegenstände in einander laufen, zu ver-
gleichen ist." Schopenhauer, *Werke*, II, 159.

16. Shopenhauer, *Werke*, II, 222–224, 230, 240–241.

17. Schopenhauer, *Werke*, II, 150.

# ELSE VON DER TANNE

oder

Das Glück Domini Friedemann Leutenbachers, armen Dieners
am Wort Gottes zu Wallrode im Elend

# ELSA OF THE FOREST

or

The Happiness of Master Friedemann Leutenbacher, Poor Minister
of the Word of God at Wallrode in Elend

Es schneiete heftig, und es hatte fast den ganzen Tag hindurch geschneit. Als es Abend werden wollte, verstärkte sich die Heftigkeit des Sturmes; das Gestäube und Gewirbel um die Hütten des Dorfes schien nimmer ein Ende nehmen zu wollen; verweht wurden Weg und Steg. Im wilden Harzwald, nicht weit von dessen Rande die armen Hütten in einem Häuflein zusammengekauert lagen, sauste und brauste es mächtig. Es knackte das Gezweig, es knarrten die Stämme; der Wolf heulte, wenn die Windsbraut eine kurze Minute lang Atem schöpfte;—man schrieb den Vierundzwanzigsten Decembris im Jahr eintausendsechshundertundachtundvierzig.

Dominus Magister Friedemann Leutenbacher, der Pfarrherr zu Wallrode im Elend, hatte den ganzen Tag über an seiner Weihnachtspredigt gearbeitet und Speise und Trank, ja schier jegliches Aufblicken darob versäumt; das irdische Leben war so bitter, daß man es nur ertragen konnte, indem man es vergaß; aber der Prediger im Elend konnte es nicht vergessen: eine *solche* Weihnachtsrede hatte er noch nicht schreiben müssen. Er war nicht alt, der Pfarrherr zu Wallrode; er war im Jahre sechzehnhundertzehn geboren; allein dreißig Jahre seines Daseins mochten dreifach und vierfach gerechnet werden; eine solche Zeit des Greuels und der Verwüstung hatte die Welt nicht gesehen, seit das Imperium Romanum versank vor den wandernden Völkern. Nun war das zweite Imperium, das Römische Reich Deutscher Nation, auch zerbrochen, und wenngleich die Ruine zur Verwunderung aller Welt noch durch hundertundfünfzig Jahre aufrecht stand, so lösten sich doch bei jedem Sturm und Wind verwitterte, morsche Teile ab und stürzten mit Gekrach hernieder. So war es geschehen, als man den Frieden zu Münster und Osnabrück schloß, und zwei Drittel der Nation waren verschüttet worden durch den Dreißigjährigen Krieg.

Ehrn Friedemann Leutenbacher, der Pastor zu Wallrode im Elend, wußte davon zu sagen. Um seine Handgelenke trug er die blutigroten Spuren und Striemen der Stricke und Riemen, welche ihm die Raubgesellen des General Pfuhl, der sich rühmte,

It was snowing violently, and it had been snowing almost the entire day. As evening began to draw on, the violence of the storm increased; the eddying of the snow-dust about the huts of the village seemed as if it would never cease; road and path were obscured by drifting snow. In the wild Harz Forest, not far from whose edge the wretched huts lay huddled together in a small group, the storm blustered and roared mightily. The branches crackled; the tree-trunks creaked. The wolf howled whenever the gale paused a brief moment for breath. It was the twenty-fourth of December in the year one thousand six hundred and forty-eight.

Master Friedemann Leutenbacher, the pastor of Wallrode in Elend, had worked throughout the entire day on his Christmas sermon, and he had neglected food and drink, indeed had even neglected to look up from his work on that account. Life on this earth was so bitter that it could be endured only by forgetting it. But the preacher in Elend was unable to forget it; never before had he had to write such a Christmas address. He was not old, the pastor of Wallrode; he had been born in the year sixteen hundred and ten; but thirty years of existence might well have been counted three or four times over. The world had not witnessed such a time of horror and devastation since the *Imperium Romanum* fell before the roving hordes. Now the second *Imperium*, the Roman Empire of the German Nation, had also been shattered; and although, to the astonishment of all the world, its ruins still stood erect for a hundred and fifty years longer, with every storm and wind, nevertheless, mouldering and decaying parts fell away and tumbled down with a crash. So had it happened when peace was concluded at Muenster and Osnabrueck and two-thirds of the nation had been destroyed by the Thirty Years' War.

The Reverend Friedemann Leutenbacher, the pastor of Wallrode in Elend, could tell of that from his own experience. Around his wrists he bore the blood-red marks and welts of cord and thong which the brigands of General Pfuhl, who boasted of

allein achthundert Dörfer verbrannt zu haben, anlegten, als sie
ihn zwischen den Gäulen fortschleppten in den Wald. Des Gallas barbarisch Volk hatte ihn den schwedischen Trunk probieren
lassen, und was Linnard Torstensons fliegende Scharen an seinem armen Leibe und an seinen Pfarrkindern verübt hatten,
das war nicht auszureden.

Es schneiete heftig, und es schien nimmer ein Ende nehmen zu
können; die Dämmerung aber nahm wohl eine Stunde zu früh
dem schreibenden Magister die Feder aus der Hand; es war ihm,
als ob sie auch leise und unmerklich in sein Hirn gekrochen sei,
als er aufblickte und einen Blick um sich her und durch das
Fenster warf.

Da lag vor ihm der schlechte Fetzen groben Papieres, mit welchem letztern er in seiner Einsamkeit so sparsam umgehen
mußte, da lagen die wenigen Bücher, welche der höhnischen Zer-
störungslust der wilden streifenden Rotten entgangen waren,
da lag vor allem die alte, zerfetzte Bibel, welche er im Jahre
1639 aus dem dritten Brande seiner Hütte gerettet hatte und
welche an ihrem Einband und dem Rande der vergilbten Blätter Zeichen der leckenden Flammen trug: und alles das Rüst-
zeug des Geistes war, seiner Äußerlichkeit nach, im vollkomme-
nen Einklang mit allem, was den Pfarrer sonst umgab. Die
schlechteste Hütte jetziger Zeit hätte mehr Gegenstände und
Hülfsmittel der Üppigkeit aufzuweisen als dieses Pastorenhaus,
auf dessen Dach der rote Hahn dreimal während dieses scheuß-
lichen Kriegs gesessen hatte, und nur die große weiße Katze,
welche im Winkel neben dem Herde zusammengerollt lag,
mochte sich behaglich darin fühlen.

Aber der Pfarrherr sah nichts von der Trostlosigkeit, die ihn
umgab; er war im Elend aufgewachsen, und „Im Elend" hieß
die hungerige Waldgegend, in welcher sein Pfarrdorf lag. Nur
ein einziges Mal in seinem Leben hatte er während seiner Schul-
zeit zu Wittenberg freier Atem holen können; aber der Sonnen-
blick war so schnell vorübergeflogen, daß es wie ein ferner, ferner, unbestimmter Traum erscheinen mußte;—im Elend wäre

162

having alone burned eight hundred villages, had laid on him when they dragged him off into the forest between two horses. The barbaric followers of Gallas had made him try the "Swedish drink," and the things that Linnard Torstenson's flying troops had practiced on his miserable body and on those of his parishioners were beyond telling.

It was snowing violently, and it seemed as if it could never end. The twilight caused the writing scholar to lay aside his pen fully an hour too soon. As he looked up, casting a glance around him and through the window, he felt as if the twilight had crept softly and imperceptibly into his brain as well.

There before him lay the wretched scrap of coarse paper, of which he had to be so sparing in his solitude. There lay the few books which had escaped the scornful destructiveness of the wild roving raiders. Above all there lay the ancient and tattered Bible which he had salvaged from the third burning of his hut in the year sixteen hundred and thirty-nine, and which bore evidence of the lambent flames on its binding and on the edge of its gilt leaves. And all the armor of the spirit was from its appearance in perfect harmony with the other surroundings of the minister. The most miserable hut of the present day could boast more objects and means of luxury than this parsonage, on whose roof the red cock of fire had thrice alighted during this hideous war. And only the large white cat that lay nestled in the corner beside the hearth might feel comfortable in it.

But the pastor saw nothing of his disconsolate surroundings; he had grown up in misery, and the name of the hungry forest district in which his parish village lay meant "in misery." Only once in his life, during his student years at Wittenberg, had he been able to breathe more freely; that glimpse of sunshine, however, had vanished so quickly that it could but appear as a far away and nebulous dream. Friedemann Leutenbacher would,

Friedemann Leutenbacher längst verlorengegangen, wie das
deutsche Volk, wenn Else von der Tanne nicht gewesen wäre.

Er hatte die Feder neben seiner Weihnachtspredigt niederge-
legt, trat zu dem niedern Fenster und betrachtete in der Dämmerung die roten Narben um seine Handgelenke. Er war sehr
betrübt und dachte, während er so stand, wie das deutsche Volk
gleich ihm mit gefesselten Händen, zerschlagen und blutig, herausgeschleppt sei und niedergeworfen. Der Herr hatte gebrüllt
aus der Höhe und seinen Donner hören lassen aus seiner heiligen Wohnung; er hatte ein Lied gesungen wie die Weintreter,
über alle Bewohner des Landes; sein Hall war erschollen bis an
der Welt Ende; und bis an der Welt Ende lagen die Erschlagenen und wurden nicht geklaget noch aufgehoben noch begraben.
Ehrn Friedemann Leutenbacher aber dachte noch viel mehr an
Else von der Tanne, welche jetzt aus dem großen Walde fort-
gehen mußte, und er sprach mit den Worten des Propheten an
diesem Abend vor Weihnachten des Jahres sechzehnhundertachtundvierzig:

„Er hat mein Fleisch und meine Haut alt gemacht und mein
Gebein zerschlagen.

Er hat mich verbauet und mich mit Galle und Mühe umgeben.

Er hat mich in Finsternis gelegt, wie die Toten in der Welt.

Er hat mich vermauert, daß ich nicht herauskann, und mich in
harte Fesseln gelegt."

Dann seufzte er tief und schwer; durch das Gestöber im Dunkel glimmerten zwei order drei Lichter seines Dorfes, doch da er
wußte, welche tierische Verdummung, welche Schmach und welcher Jammer des Menschen um diese matten Flämmchen kauer-
ten, so wandte sich sein Geist auch von ihnen ab, um angstvoll
suchend weiterzuirren; und immer finsterer ward die Nacht,
immer heftiger der Sturm.

Die weiße Katze war aufgestanden, schlich durch die Stube,
miauzte und kam, sich an den Beinen ihres Herrn zu reiben;
Martina sah in das Gemach und fragte, ob sie die Lampe an-
zünden solle; aber der Pfarrer schüttelte den Kopf und sagte

163

like the German people, have long since been lost in misery, had it not been for Else von der Tanne.

He put down his pen beside his Christmas sermon and stepped to the low-silled window, observing in the twilight the red scars around his wrists. He was very downcast and reflected as he stood there how the German people, like him, with chained hands, had been beaten down, dragged out amid blood and prostrated. The Lord had roared from on high and uttered his voice from his holy habitation; He had given a shout, as they that tread the grapes, against all the inhabitants of the earth, and its noise had come even to the ends of the earth; and as far as the ends of the earth lay the slain, without mourning or care or burial. But the Reverend Friedemann Leutenbacher thought even more about Else von der Tanne, who had now to leave the great forest, and he spoke with the words of the prophet on this Christmas Eve of the year sixteen hundred and forty-eight:

"My flesh and my skin hath He made old; He hath broken my bones. He hath builded against me, and compassed me with gall and travail. He hath set me in dark places as them that be dead in the world. He hath hedged me about that I cannot get out; He hath made my chain heavy."

Then he sighed deeply and heavily. In the dark, two or three lights of his village glimmered through the driving snow; yet because he knew what brute apathy, what ignominy, and what wretchedness of human beings cowered about these feeble little flames, his mind turned from these also only to sink deeper into grief and anxiety. Darker and darker became the night; more and more violent became the storm.

The white cat, which had stood up, now crept through the chamber, miaowed, and came over to rub itself against the legs of its master. Martina glanced into the room and asked if she should light the lamp; but the minister shook his head and said, "No."

nein;—Martina machte leise die Tür wieder zu; Ehrn Friedemann Leutenbacher blickte immer noch hinaus in die Dunkel-
heit, er dachte immer noch an Else von der Tanne, und seine
Seele war gefangener denn je.

Er dachte an Else von der Tanne, an ihre Hütte neben der
hohen Tanne, an den sonnigen Sommertag, an welchem der Magister Konradus sein sechsjähriges Kind auf dem Arm in den
Wald getragen hatte. Er dachte an ihre Stimme im Walde, er
dachte daran, wie sie im Dickicht sang und Kränze wand, und
dann dachte er daran, wie seine Pfarrkinder das schöne Mädchen für eine Hexe hielten, ihr auswichen, wenn sie ihr allein
begegneten, sie verhöhnten, verspotteten und verfolgten, wenn
eine Schar von ihnen im wilden Forst auf sie traf; er dachte an
den Tag Sankt Johannis des Täufers und stöhnte laut und rang
die Hände.

Es war eine so seltsame, so wunderliche Geschichte. Bannier
hatte am vierundzwanzigsten September sechzehnhundertsechs-
unddreißig die Sachsen und Kaiserlichen bei Wittstock in grim-
migster Feldschlacht geschlagen und war Herr in Deutschland.
Achtzigtausend Feinde erwürgte er, und sechshundert Fahnen
und Standarten gewann er während seiner Kriegführung; aber
das Volk nannte schaudernd die Jahre seines Kommandos die
„Schwedenzeit", und durch die Jahrhunderte klingt der unsäg-
liche Jammer, den dieses Wort bedeutet, leise und schaurig fort.

In der Schwedenzeit erschien Else mit ihrem Vater zu Wallrode im Elend.

Es kamen Kinder, die gegen Ende des Septembers im Walde
Holz gelesen hatten, heim und erzählten, an der hohen Tanne
halte ein wunderlich Wesen, ein Gefährt, gezogen von einem
schwarzen Roß und bewacht von einem wilden, gewaffneten
Mann und vier Hunden, groß und grimm wie Wölfe. Und sie
berichteten weiter, es sei ein Feuer angezündet unter der hohen
Tanne, und neben dem Feuer sitze ein Mägdlein ganz holdselig,
und der wilde Mann koche ihm ein Süppchen.

Da machten sich einige aus dem Dorfe auf, das fremde Wesen

164

Martina closed the door softly again. The Reverend Friedemann Leutenbacher continued to gaze out into the darkness; he kept thinking of Else von der Tanne, and his soul became more oppressed than ever.

He thought of Else von der Tanne, of her hut beside the tall fir tree, of the sunny summer's day when Master Conrad had carried his six-year-old child on his arm into the forest. He thought of her voice in the forest; he thought of how she sang in the thicket and wove garlands. And then he recalled how his parishioners had believed the lovely girl to be a witch, and shunned her whenever they met her alone, but scorned, mocked, and pursued her whenever a group of them chanced upon her in the wild forest. He thought of St. John the Baptist's day and groaned aloud and wrung his hands.

It was such a strange, such a wondrous story. On the twenty-fourth of September sixteen hundred and thirty-six, Bannier had defeated the Saxons and Imperials at Wittstock in a most fierce pitched battle, and was lord and master in Germany. He massacred eighty thousand of the enemy and captured six hundred flags and standards during his campaign. But the people, shuddering, called the years of his command the "Swedish period" and down through the centuries softly and terribly resounds the unspeakable misery which those words imply.

It was in the Swedish period that Else appeared with her father at Wallrode in Elend.

Toward the end of that September, children, returning home from gathering wood in the forest, related how a strange object had stopped in the forest by the tall fir-tree, a cart drawn by a black horse and guarded by a wild, armed man and four dogs as large and fierce as wolves. And they reported further that a fire had been kindled under the tall fir-tree, and beside the fire sat a most gracious little girl while the man cooked a broth for her.

Then some set out from the village to see the strange

auch zu sehen, und kehrten zurück und sagten aus, es sei also, das Feuer brenne und die vier Hunde seien auch vorhanden und das Mägdlein habe den Kopf auf den Leib des einen gelegt und schlafe, das schwarze Roß weide im Gebüsch und der fremde Mann haue Gestrüpp und baue eine Hütte für die Nacht, es seien aber keine Tartaren.

Da ging auch der junge Pfarrer Friedemann Leutenbacher in den Wald hinaus und fand alles so, wie man ihm erzählt hatte; doch sah er nicht gleich den andern scheu aus der Ferne auf die Fremden, sondern er trat an sie heran, grüßte den finstern bärtigen Mann und wollte ihn fragen, weshalb er hier in der unfreundlichen Wildnis sein Nachtlager aufschlage und weshalb er nicht hinab ins Dorf und in das Pastorenhaus gestiegen sei, um mit dem vorliebzunehmen, was das Dorf im Elend bieten könne und die böse Zeit übriggelassen habe. Der fremde Mann jedoch erwiderte den frommen Gruß nicht, er sah nicht auf von seiner Arbeit, und die langen wüsten Haare verhingen ihm das Gesicht. Nur das schwarze Roß sah auf den Pastor, und drei von den greulichen Hunden richteten sich empor, reckten sich, knurrten und wiesen ihre weißen Zähne und blutroten Zungen. Der vierte, auf dessen struppigem Leibe das Köpfchen des schlafenden Kindes lag, blieb liegen; aber auch er murrte und wies die Zähne; der Pfarrer wußte nicht, was er ferner sagen und tun sollte; er stand zweifelnd und sah zu, wie unter den kunstfertigen Händen des Fremden die Hütte aus Gestrüpp und Gezweig sich erhob; er sah auf das zweiräderige Fuhrwerk und auf das niederglimmende Feuer neben der hohen Tanne. Vor allem aber sah er auf das schlafende Mägdlein, welches plötzlich ein Strahl der abendlichen Sonne, in rötlichem Glanz um den Stamm einer uralten Eiche schießend, traf und welches nunmehr in diesem Glanz und Blenden die Augen aufschlug. Es reckte sich auch und richtete sich empor, und in demselben Augenblick schoß der Wolfshund, dessen Leib ihm zum Kopfkissen gedient hatte, auf und fuhr mit Geheul gegen den Pfarrer.

Da rief das Kind lieblich erschreckt:

165

sight for themselves and returned saying that it was true; the
fire was burning and the four dogs were there also; the little girl
had laid her head on the body of one of them and was sleeping;
the black horse was grazing in the bushes; and the strange man
was hewing underbrush and building a hut for the night. But they
were not gypsies.

Thereupon the young minister, Friedemann Leutenbacher,
also went out into the forest and found everything just as he had
been told. But he did not observe the strangers shyly from a
distance like the others; he approached them and greeted the
somber bearded man with the intention of asking him why he
was pitching his camp for the night here in the unfriendly wilderness, and why he had not come down into the village and to the
parsonage to put up with what little the village in Elend had to
offer that was left to it by the bad times. But the strange man did
not return the friendly greeting. He did not even look up from
his work while his long dishevelled hair concealed his face. Only
the black horse looked at the pastor, and three of the savage dogs
straightened up, stretched themselves, and snarled showing their
white teeth and blood-red tongues. The fourth, on whose shaggy
body the little hand of the sleeping child rested, did not stir; but
he too growled and bared his teeth. The minister did not know
what further to say or do. Perplexed, he stood by, and watched
the hut arise from the underbrush and branches under the skillful
hand of the stranger. He observed the two-wheeled vehicle and
the waning fire beside the tall fire-tree. But above all he observed
the sleeping maid upon whom a ray of the evening sun suddenly
fell, projected in a reddish brilliancy around the trunk of a prime-
val oak. By this time she had opened her eyes in this effulgence
and brilliancy. She too stretched herself, and sat up. At the same
moment the wolf-hound whose body had served her as a pillow
shot up and charged howling at the pastor.

The child cried, charmingly frightened,

„Marschalk! Marschalk! zurück! laß ab!"

Und Marschalk nahm die Vorderpfoten von der Brust des Pfarrherrn und ging zu den drei bösen Genossen; das Mägdlein erhob sich aber von der Erde, lächelte und trat auf Ehrn Friedemann Leutenbacher zu und sagte:

„Einen fröhlichen Abend wünsch ich dir! Er hat dich wohl schwer erschreckt, der arme Marschalk? Zürn ihm nicht, ich bitt dich."

Sie wollte noch mehr sagen, und der Pastor von Wallrode im Elend wollte ihr antworten; da schritt aber der bärtige Mann mit seiner Axt her, faßte den Arm des Kindes, stellte sich dräuend vor den Pfarrherrn und schob ihn mit dem Stiel der Axt zurück und wies in den Wald, als wolle er sagen: Geh deines Weges, ich will nichts zu schaffen haben mit dir; ich will dein Lächeln und deine freundlichen Worte nicht! Geh hin, woher du gekommen bist, und warne dein Volk, daß es uns nicht in den Weg komme.

Die Augen des Mannes leuchteten noch viel schrecklicher als die des zornigen Hundes, da dieser sich vor der Brust Friedemanns aufrichtete; und als der Pfarrherr noch ein gut Wörtlein sagen wollte, da erhob der Fremde so dräuend das blanke Beil, daß jener erschreckt zurücktrat, um dem Schlage auszuweichen.

Das kleine Mädchen schrie auf und bedeckte die Augen mit den Händchen, und Ehrn Friedemann Leutenbacher, als er sah, daß sein guter Wille also verachtet werde, schritt seines Weges durch den Forst zurück, in tiefen Gedanken, und sprach daheim seinem Völklein zu, man möge den Fremden in Frieden gewähren und ziehen lassen; es sei eine Zeit Gottes, in welcher der Herr der Menschen Sinnen und Gedanken, Tun und Treiben arg durcheinanderworfele auf seiner Tenne, eine Zeit, in welcher ein jeglicher, es sei Mann oder Weib, so viel mit sich selber zu tun habe, daß ein jeglicher wohltue, für sein armes Teil Frieden zu halten und jedem armen Bruder seinen Weg offenzulassen.

Die Gemeinde schüttelte die Köpfe; aber sie mußte wohl dem Wort ihres geistlichen Beraters folgen, fürchtete sich auch wohl

166

"Marshal, Marshal, back! Stop it!"

And Marshal dropped his forepaws from the breast of the pastor and joined his three angry companions. But the little girl arose from the ground, smiled, and approached the Reverend Friedemann Leutenbacher, saying,

"Good evening to you, sir. Did he really frighten you badly, poor Marshal? Don't be angry with him, please."

She was on the point of saying more, and the pastor of Wallrode in Elend on the point of answering her, but the bearded man, stepping forward with his axe, grasped the arm of his child, placed himself threateningly before the pastor, and pushed him back with the helve of his axe. He pointed into the forest as if to say, "Go your way. I will have nothing to do with you. I do not want your smile or your friendly words. Return whence you came, and warn your people to stay out of our way."

The eyes of the man gleamed even more terribly than those of the angry dog, as the latter sprang up before the breast of Friedemann, and just as the pastor was about to say another friendly word or two, the stranger lifted the gleaming axe so threateningly that the former drew back, frightened, to avoid the blow.

The little girl cried aloud, and covered her eyes with her small hands. Seeing how his good will was thus scorned, Friedemann Leutenbacher retraced his steps through the forest sunk in deep thought. At home again he counselled his people to leave the stranger in peace to come and go; it was a time of God, he said, in which he was winnowing the schemes and thoughts, the deeds and strivings of men in a bewildering manner on His threshing-floor. It was a time in which everyone, man or woman, had so many personal problems that each would do well to keep peace for his own small part and to let every poor fellow-man go his own way.

The parishioners shook their heads; but indeed the words of their spiritual adviser had to be heeded, and then too some

ein wenig vor den vier starken Hunden und dem Feuergewehr
des wilden Fremdlings, vermeinte auch, daß der letztere mit
allem, was er mit sich führe, gehen werde, wie er gekommen sei,
sintemalen er doch nicht hausen könne unter der hohen Tanne
im Elend.

Als aber am andern Tage neugierige Seelen wieder zur hohen
Tanne schlichen, da fanden sie das Wesen noch am alten Ort; sie
hörten die Hunde in der Ferne bellen und vernahmen einen
Büchsenkrach und sahen den unheimlichen Mann mit einem er-
legten Rehbock aus dem Gebüsch kommen, das Kind sahen sie
nicht; und darnach regnete es wohl zwei Wochen, und niemand
kam so weit in den Wald; in der dritten Woche jedoch stieg der
Fremdling, mit seiner Büchse auf der Schulter, begleitet von
einem der Hunde, in das Dorf hinab und setzte sich vor dem
verbrannten Gemeindehaus auf einen Haufen verkohlter Balken. Da dauerte es nicht lange, daß das Volk aus den Hütten
sich in einem weiten Kreis um ihn her versammelt hatte, und
ein Knab lief zum Pfarrherrn, um ihm anzuzeigen, was sich be-
geben habe und wie der Mann von der hohen Tanne gleich
einem Tauben und Stummen vor dem Rathaus sitze. Mit Wunder erhub sich nun auch der Pastor von seiner Arbeit, trat auf
die Gasse und ging mit dem Boten zum Gemeindeplatz, fand
auch, daß es so war, wie ihm mit fliegendem Atem berichtet
worden war.

Als der Fremde seiner ansichtig wurde, stand er schnell auf,
schritt dem Pfarrherrn entgegen und lüftete ein wenig den Filz-
hut, bot sodann ganz höflich die Zeit und sprach auf lateinisch:

„Domine, mich verlanget, dir zu sagen, daß es mir leid ist um
den Tag, an welchem wir zuerst uns sahen. Die Zeit sprach aus
mir und mein Schicksal; verzeihe mir. Non sum impostor nec
proditor nec erro nec magus nec thraso, ich bin kein Betrüger
oder Verräter, kein Landstreicher oder Schwarzkünstler, kein
Schnarchhans. Ich bin ein Sohn deines Volkes und wie das
Vaterland im Elend. Ich komme aus der Ferne und will bei
euch wohnen, will eine Hütte im Walde bauen für mein Kind—

                                                                  167

were not a little afraid of the four powerful dogs and the firearm of the wild stranger. It was also supposed that the latter would depart with everything that he had brought with him, just as he had come, since after all he surely could not lodge under the tall fir tree in Elend.

When, however, curious persons stole out again the next day to the tall fir tree, they found things there the same: they heard the dogs barking in the distance and the report of a rifle. They watched the uncanny man emerge from the thicket with a slain roebuck, but they did not see the child. Thereafter it rained about two weeks, and no one ventured so far into the forest. In the third week, however, the stranger, with his rifle on his shoulder and accompanied by one of his dogs, descended into the village, and sat down in front of the burned town-hall on a pile of charred beams. It was not long before the people had come out of their huts and gathered in a large circle around him. A boy ran to the pastor to inform him of what had taken place: how the man from the tall fir tree was sitting as if deaf and dumb in front of the townhall. Now the pastor too arose astonished from his work, stepped into the street, and went with the messenger to the town-square, and found that it was just as it had been breathlessly related to him.

When the stranger saw him, he stood up quickly, and approached the pastor, tipping his felt hat slightly; he then wished him a good day, speaking in Latin:

"*Domine*, I want to say to you that I am sorry about the day when we first met. The times and my fate caused me to speak in such a way. Forgive me. *Non sum impostor, nec proditor, nec error, nec magus, nec thraso.* I am no swindler or traitor, no vagabond or magician, no braggart. I am a son of your people, and like the fatherland, I am in distress. I come from far away and desire to live among you; I want to build a hut in the forest for my child.

hilf mir, daß es so geschehe, ich will es auch den Leuten deines Dorfes lohnen."

Staunend über solche Rede hub der junge Pfarrherr die Hände; diese Sprache hatte er nicht erwarten können. Sie trug den Fremden so hoch hinaus über die armen Menschen, unter welchen der Prediger bis jetzt seine Tage verbringen mußte, daß Ehrn Friedemannn fast die Antwort vergaß und sich erst besann, als ihn der Fremde recht ungeduldig ansah. Nun redete auch er in lateinischer Zunge zu dem Fremden und meinte, hocherfreulich müsse ihm die Ankunft und Absicht eines solchen Mannes sein; doch verwunderlich erscheine letztere ihm auch. Der Winter sei vor der Tür; und hart, rauh und langdauernd sei er in diesem Gebirge, und es sei doch wohl nicht gut und barmherzig, ein zart klein Kind allen Gefahren und Beschwerden der Wildnis auszusetzen. Das Dorf sei arm, sprach der Pfarrherr, und habe arg und viel gelitten von der langen, schrecklichen Kriegesnot, doch biete es zuletzt immer noch einen bessern Schutz und Zufluchtsort als der wilde Forst; es stehe mehr denn eine Hütte leer, deren solle der Herr die Wahl haben, und er—Friedemann Leutenbacher—wolle in allem helfen und zu Rat und Handen sein, wo und wie er könne.

Auf diese Rede schüttelte der Fremde nur den Kopf und antwortete, er sei dankbar, doch sein Entschluß stehe fest; sein Sinn sei nicht angetan, unter den Menschen zu wohnen, sein Kind aber müsse bei ihm hausen im Wald und könne es auch.

Ganz verdutzt hatten die Bauern von Wallrode während dieses Zwiegesprächs dagestanden. Ihre Blicke wanderten zwischen ihrem Pfarrherrn und dem Fremden hin und her, sie kratzten sich hinter den Ohren und stießen einander in die Seiten und schlossen ihren Kreis immer enger. Jetzt aber setzte ihnen Ehrn Friedemann Leutenbacher auseinander, was der fremde Mann wünsche und verlange, und nun erhob sich ein Gemurmel in der Gemeinde, welches allmählich zum lauten Geschrei wurde.

Die einen sagten, man müsse dem ausländischen Herrn helfen,

Help me to do it, and I will even repay the people of your village."

Astonished by such speech, the young pastor raised his hands; he should not have expected such language. It elevated the stranger so high above the poor people among whom the preacher had had until now to spend his days that the Reverend Friedemann almost forgot to answer, and only bethought himself as the stranger regarded him somewhat impatiently. Now he too spoke in the Latin tongue to the stranger, saying that the arrival and intention of such a man must needs be a great pleasure for him; yet his intention, continued the pastor, did seem amazing even to him. Winter was approaching and it was hard, bleak, and persistent in these mountains; and further, it was hardly kind and merciful to expose a small and tender child to the dangers and privations of the wilderness. The village was poor, said the curate, and had suffered much and sorely from the long terrible stress of war; yet after all it still offered better shelter and refuge than the wild forest. There was more than one hut standing empty; of these the gentleman should have the choice, and he, Friedmann Leutenbacher, would help in all things and be of assistance whenever he could.

At this speech the stranger only shook his head, rejoining that he was grateful, but his decision was firm; he was not disposed to live among men; his child, moreover, had to dwell with him in the forest and she was well able to do so.

During this dialogue the peasants of Wallrode had stood quite dumbfounded. Their glances kept shifting from their pastor to the stranger and back again. They scratched themselves behind the ears, nudged one another, and drew their circle closer and closer. But now the Reverend Friedmann Leutenbacher explained to them what the strange man desired, whereupon there arose a murmuring in the crowd that gradually grew into a loud clamor.

Some said that they should help the foreign gentleman,

da er Geld biete und wenig verlange; die andern vermeinten, dem Ding sei nicht zu trauen, und das Wesen gefalle ihnen gar nicht. Letztere hatten den Kopf voll von allerlei unheimlichen Bedenken und meinten, sie traueten niemandem mehr, nicht dem Nachbar, nicht dem Verwandten, ja kaum noch dem Herrgott. Sie fluchten, wenn sie an die erduldeten Leiden und das gegenwärtige Elend dachten, und sie waren leider so im Recht, daß sie niemand darum strafen konnte.

Man könne nicht wissen, sagten sie, welchem neuen Unheil dieser fremde Mensch mit seiner seltsamlichen Begleitung vorangehe. Die Welt sei nun einmal wie ausgewechselt und so falsch, schlecht und blutig, daß ein jeglicher sich hüten solle und daß keiner mehr auf sich lade, als er müsse.

Sie redeten noch mancherlei und erhitzten sich immer mehr, bis sie wieder vor den begütigenden Worten des Pfarrherrn still wurden. Das Ende vom Widerstreit aber war, daß man den Fremden aufforderte, seinen Namen, Stand und früheren Wohnort anzugeben und darzutun, in welcher Weiser er imstande sei, den guten Willen und die Hülfleistung des Dorfes Wallrode im Elend zu erkaufen.

Da sprach der Mann, er wolle sich nennen der Magister Konradus, mehr aber sei nicht zu wissen nötig, und werde er auch nichts weiter sagen. Was aber den zweiten Punkt anbelange, so solle man angeben, was man fordere für das, was er wünsche, nämlich eine Hütte und Frieden.

Als er bei diesen Worten in die Ledertasche an seiner Seite griff und vier Goldstücke hervorzog und sie in der hohlen Hand zeigte, da stießen die Bauern die Köpfe zusammen und berieten von neuem. Die Vorsichtigen, die Furchtsamen und die Schreier wurden überstimmt; es wurde beschlossen, dem Magister Konradus die erbetene Hülfe zu leisten und ihn an der hohen Tanne in Frieden wohnen zu lassen, solange er selber Frieden halte.

Besiegelt wurde der Pakt durch einen Handschlag zwischen dem Pfarrherrn Friedemann Leutenbacher und dem Fremden, die Hütte wurde erbaut aus altem Gebälk und Brettern, aus

since he offered money and wanted but little in return. Others were of the opinion that the proposal was not to be trusted, and the matter pleased them not at all. The latter had their heads full of all sorts of sinister misgivings, and said they no longer trusted anyone, not even a neighbor or relative, indeed hardly even the Heavenly Father. They cursed whenever they thought of the suffering they had endured and of their present misery. And they were, alas, so justified that no one could blame them for it.

It was impossible to know, they said, what new disaster might precede this strange man with his singular entourage. The world was turned so upside down anyway and was so false, wicked, and bloody that everyone should look out for himself, and no one should take more upon himself than he had to.

Much discussion followed and the villagers became more and more excited until they were again pacified by the soothing words of the pastor. The upshot of the dispute, however, was that the stranger was enjoined to disclose his name, profession, and former place of residence, and to prove in what way he would be able to pay for the good will and assistance of the village of Wallrode in Elend.

Thereupon the man replied that he preferred to be called Master Conrad; it was not necessary to know more than that and as a matter of fact he would say no more. As to the second point, however, it should be made clear what would be asked for what he desired, namely, a hut and peace.

When at these words he reached into the leather wallet on his side and took out four pieces of gold, showing them in the palm of his hand, the peasants put their heads together and deliberated anew. The cautious and timid ones, as well as the clamorers, were outvoted. It was decided to render Master Conrad the requested aid and to allow him to live under the tall fir-tree in peace as long as he himself was peaceful.

The compact was sealed by a handshake between the pastor, Friedemann Leutenbacher, and the stranger. The hut was built from old beams and boards,

Rasen und Steinen—ein wüstes Ding, selbst solang es noch neu
war. Der Magister Konradus aber wohnte in der Hütte an der
hohen Tanne mit seinem Kind, und die vier gewaltigen Hunde
hielten Wacht davor. Das schwarze Roß stand unter einem
Wetterdach.——

Zwölf lange, unruhevolle, mühselige, martervolle Jahre war's
her, und es ist schon gesagt, wie die Welt, das Dorf Wallrode im
Elend und der Pfarrer zu Wallrode, Ehrn Friedemann Leutenbacher, während dieser Zeit gelitten hatten. Aber über die ver-
borgene Stelle im wilden Walde, über die Hütte an der hohen
Tanne, in welcher der Magister Konradus mit seinem Kinde
lebte, hatte das Geschick schützend seine Hand gehalten. Wie
oft auch die Kriegsfurie diesen abgelegenen Erdenwinkel mit
ihren Schrecken erreicht hatte: die Hütte an der hohen Tanne
war stehengeblieben, und ihre einzigen Feinde waren die Jahre
und die Witterung gewesen; die Leute aus dem Dorfe hatten es
nicht gewagt, sie niederzulegen, obgleich sie oft genug den besten
und bösesten Willen dazu hatten.

Nun dachte der Pfarrherr zu Wallrode im Elend, Herr Friedemann Leutenbacher, an diesem Vierundzwanzigsten des Dezem-
bers sechzehnhundertachtundvierzig in Wonne und Schmerz daran, wie viele Fäden zwischen seiner Hütte und der Hütte an
der hohen Tanne hin- und widerliefen und wie sein Leben ein
anderes geworden seit den Herbsttagen nach der blutigen Wittstocker Schlacht.

Er hatte in einer Wüste, einer Wildnis gelebt und nicht ge-
ahnet, daß es Blumen gebe in der Welt und daß der Boden dazu
geschaffen sei, sie zu tränken und zu speisen und ihre Pracht
und Schönheit als seinen Schmuck zu tragen. Nun hatte eine
Wunderhand aus fremdem Lande in die Wildnis und Wüste ein
grün Zweiglein getragen und es in die schwarze, traurige Erde
gesteckt, und Ehrn Friedemann hatte in Verwunderung gestanden und zugesehen und die Bedeutung nicht gewußt. Aber ein
jeglicher Tag, der kam, brachte dem Zweiglein sein Tröpfchen
Segen, und jeglicher Tag, der kam, tat das Seine, das Wunder

from turf and stone—a wretched affair even when it was new. But Master Conrad dwelt in the hut beside the tall fir tree with his child, and the four powerful dogs stood watch in front of it. The black horse stood under a shed.

That was twelve long, turbulent, toilsome, torturing years ago, and it has already been related how the world, the village of Wallrode in Elend, and the minister of Wallrode, the Reverend Friedemann Leutenbacher, had suffered during that time. But fate had held its protecting hand over the hidden place in the wild forest, over the hut beside the tall fir tree in which Master Conrad lived with his child. However often the fury of war had reached into this remote corner of the earth with its terrors, the hut beside the tall fir tree had remained standing, and its only enemies had been the years and the weather. The people of the village had not dared to tear it down, although they had often enough the greatest and most evil desire to do so.

Now the pastor of Wallrode in Elend, Friedemann Leuten-bacher, recalled with mingled bliss and pain on this twenty-fourth of December, sixteen hundred and forty-eight, how many ties ran back and forth between his hut and the hut beside the tall fir tree, and how his life had been transformed since the autumnal days after the bloody Wittstock battle.

He had lived in a desert, a wilderness, without suspecting that there were flowers in the world and that the earth had been created to water and nourish them and to wear their beauty and splendor as its ornament. Now a magical hand from a strange land had brought a little green shoot into the wilderness and desert, and had planted it in the black, gloomy earth. And the Reverend Friedemann had stood by in wonderment and looked on, without being conscious of what it signified. But every day that came brought the tiny shoot its drop of blessing and did its own part to bring the miracle

in der Wüste zur Vollendung zu bringen. Kein Wintersturm
hatte dem schwanken, zarten Reis etwas an; keine Windsbraut,
die den Forst mit Gewalt durchfuhr und die höchsten Tannen
und Eichen brach, durfte diesem Reislen ein Leid antun; es
wuchs in der Verborgenheit und wußte nicht, wie die Welt vor
dem Walde aussah.

Durch die Wipfel der hohen Bäume sah die linde Sonne, die
auch nichts von dem großen Kriege um den Glauben und dem
Niederfall des Reiches wußte, lächelnd hernieder; und als es
wieder einmal Frühling geworden, da war der Zauber vollendet, über Nacht war das Zweiglein zu einem Rosenstock worden und stand um und um mit veschlossenen Knospen, die des
Sommers harrten.—

Der Magister Konrad hatte sich in seiner Hütte seltsam ein-
gerichtet. Der Karren, welcher seine Habseligkeiten in den Wald
trug, schien ebenfalls ein Wunderkarren zu sein. Es befanden
sich darauf mehr Dinge, als man auf den ersten Blick glauben
konnte: Hausgerät, bunte Teppiche, Bücher und Instrumente
von wunderlicher Form, Tiegel und Gläser, die nicht zum Haus-
gebrauch dienen konnten—alles wohlverpackt. Als nun die
Bauern von Wallrode ihre Arbeit und Hülfleistung an der
hohen Tanne vollendet hatten, als die Hütte stand, zog der
Fremde ein und richtete sein Wesen darin zurecht; vergeblich
suchte er aber dabei die neugierigen Augen des Dorfes auszu-
schließen. Was er in dieser Hinsicht tun konnte, tat er freilich,
und seine vier Rüden halfen ihm natürlich wacker dabei; aber
selbst das wenige, was über seinen Haushalt unter die Leute
kam, genügte, ihnen die Köpfe mit den merkwürdigsten Phan-
tasien zu füllen. Die Übertreibung gesellte sich dazu, und die,
so nichts gesehen hatten und alles nur vom Hörensagen kann-
ten, nicht weniger als die, denen durch Zufall oder Gunst ein
Einblick gestattet worden war, trugen dunkle, bedenkliche Ge-
rüchte um, welche von Tag zu Tage, von Woche zu Woche, von
Jahr zu Jahre sich ungeheuerliches färbten und sich widriger
festhingen um die dunkeln Herde von Wallrode im Elend. Da war

171

in the desert to fruition. No winter storm harmed the frail and tender shoot; no gale, raging violently through the forest and breaking the tallest firs and oaks, was allowed to harm this tender little plant. It grew in concealment and knew nothing of how the world looked beyond the forest.

The mild sun, which also knew nothing of the great religious war and of the downfall of the empire, gleamed smilingly down through the tips of the lofty trees. And when it had once more become spring, the magic was completed; overnight the little plant had become a rosebush, and stood covered with closed buds awaiting the summer.

Master Conrad had arranged things strangely in his hut. The cart that had brought his possessions into the forest appeared likewise to be a magic cart. There were more things on it than could be believed at first glance: household utensils, varicolored carpets, books and instruments of wondrous form, crucibles and glasses that could not serve for household use—all well-packed. When the peasants of Walrode had completed their work and assistance at the tall fir-tree, when the hut had been finished, the stranger moved in and arranged his belongings in it. In so doing he tried in vain to exclude the curious eyes of the village. To this end he did what he could and to be sure his four stout mastiffs aided him. Yet even the little information concerning his household that got to the populace sufficed to fill their heads with the most remarkable imaginings. Exaggeration combined with this, and those who had seen nothing or merely knew everything from hearsay spread dark suspicious rumors abroad no less than those who by favor or fortune had glimpsed the interior of the hut. From day to day, from week to week, from year to year, the rumors became more monstrously colored and intrenched themselves more obstinately around the gloomy hearths of Wallrode in Elend. Soon

bald niemand, alt oder jung—der Pfarrherr ausgenommen—im
Dorfe, der nicht bereuete, einst seine Hand zum Aufbau der Hütte
geliehen zu haben; da war bald niemand, welcher nicht mit
Freuden seine Hand geboten hätte, sie wieder niederzuwerfen.

Die Stelle bei der hohen Tanne wurde verrufen, und was das
heißen wollte um die Zeit, als der Dreißigjährige Krieg seinem
Ende zuging das mag sich jeder deuten, der weiß, was das böse
Wort heute noch im Munde und Herzen des Volkes wiegt. Ach,
es konnte ja niemand zu Wallrode im Elend, außer dem Pfarrherrn Friedemann Leutenbacher, wissen, daß es so viele tausend
gute Gründe gab, die den Menschen mit dem, was ihm noch aus
einer bessern Zeit, von einem bessern Selbst blieb, in die Einsamkeit trieben!—Nur um Ungeheuerliches, Furchtbares, Tag-
und Lichtscheues zu brüten und zu schaffen, konnte sich der
Fremde auf solche absonderliche Weise an solchem unheimlichen
Orte verborgen haben—das war die Meinung des Dorfes.

Zuletzt fanden der Magister Konradus und sein liebliches
Kind, nachdem die Rüden bis auf den tapfern Marschalk, der
auch nicht mehr sah und nicht mehr stark war, abgestorben waren, in dem Grauen, welches sich um ihr Leben in der Verborgenheit, um die Hütte an der hohen Tanne geisterhaft legte, den
einzigen Schutz. Ja dieses Grauen gab ihnen bessern Schutz, als
der Pastor Leutenbacher mit allen seinen Ermahnungen, War-
nungen und Bitten den armen, rohen, unwissenden Seelen in seiner Gemeine abringen konnte.

Daß der Pfarrherr von dem „fremden Volk" zuerst und am
giftigsten verzaubert worden sei, wußte jedes Kind im Dorfe.
Es war ihm „angetan"; selbst Gott der Herr, der doch alle
Dinge gemacht hatte, konnte ihm kaum noch helfen.

Wahrlich lag auf dem Pfarrherrn Friedemann Leutenbacher
ein Zauber, und ein gewaltiger! Je mehr seine Nachbarn im
Elend, seine Pfarrkinder, sich mit Scheu und Abscheu von dem
Wesen im Walde abwendeten, desto mehr und heftiger fühlte
er sich dazu hingezogen, und wenn solches ein Zauber war, so
war es doch kein Wunder.

there was no one in the village, young or old, save the pastor, who did not regret having once lent his hand to the construction of the hut. There was soon no one that would not have gladly offered his hand to tear it down.

The spot near the tall fir-tree became notorious. And what that could mean at the time when the Thirty Years' War was approaching its end anyone may comprehend who knows what import that evil expression has even today in the mouth and heart of the people. Alas, there really was no one at Wallrode in Elend except the pastor, Friedemann Leutenbacher, who knew that there were a thousand good reasons which could drive a man into solitude with what he had salvaged from a better time, from a better self. The stranger—so ran the opinion of the village— could have hidden himself in such an uncommon way in such a mysterious place only in order to concoct monstrous and dread-ful things—things that could not bear the light of day.

Finally, after all the mastiffs had died off except the brave Marshal, who could no longer see and was no longer strong, Mas-ter Conrad and his lovely child found protection only in the awe which had grown up ghost-like around their life in conceal-ment, around the hut beside the tall fir-tree. In fact, this awe gave them better protection than Pastor Leutenbacher could wrest from the poor, rough, ignorant souls in his parish, with all his admonishings, warnings, and pleas.

Every child in the village knew that the minister had from the outset been enchanted worst of all by the "strange folk." He was bewitched! Even God the Father, who had made all things, could scarcely help him any longer.

Verily an enchantment did possess the Reverend Friedemann Leutenbacher. And a powerful one it was! The more his neigh-bors in Elend, his parishioners, avoided the life in the forest with dread and abhorrence, so much the more powerfully did he feel himself attracted to it; and if such were an enchantment, it was no wonder.

Der Pfarrer im Elend hatte, im Gegensatz zu seiner Zeit, immerdar aufs innigste mit der Natur verkehrt; der Arme hatte ja aus seinem und seiner Umgebung Jammer nie eine andere Zufluchtsstätte gehabt als den Wald, und wenn er wenig wußte von der gelehrten Kunst, jedes schöne Leben in Forst und Feld zu zergliedern und bei seinem lateinischen oder griechischen Namen zu nennen, so hielt er sich an die Namen, die Adam den Dingen gegeben, und ließ sie in jedweder Stimmung nach Adams Weise auf sich wirken. Er sah die Zeiten des Jahres—er sah den Nebel, den Regen, den Schnee, den Sonnen- und Mondenschein kommen und gehen. Er lehnte am knorrigen Stamme der Eiche im Schatten und blickte in das glänzende Land, dessen Brand- und Blutstätten, dessen verwüstete Felder und Fluren in der allgemeinen Schönheit, welche der Mensch der Erde, seinem theatro, nimmer zu nehmen vermag, verschwanden und untergingen. Er lag den sonnigen Tag über im Gras am Bergeshang und blickte über die schwarzen Lettern seines Neuen Testamentes in die geheimnisvolle Finsternis seines Tannenwaldes und hörte die Tannen leise singen im Hauch des Windes. Weithin war er mit seiner Gegend vertraut, und jeden Fels und Stein, jeden Quell, jeden dunkelklaren Weiher im Forst kannte er und kam zu ihnen, mit ihnen zu verkehren wie mit Freunden und Verwandten—heute mit diesem, morgen mit dem, wie sein Herz und die bange oder leichtere Stimmung des Tages ihn trieben. Den dritten Teil seiner Predigten verfertigte er im Walde—er trug seine Seele hinein und gab sie ihm.

Aber wenn der Mensch seine Seele gibt, so muß er auch eine Seele wieder empfangen, wenn sich nicht der hohe Segen zum bittersten Unheil verkehren soll, und es ist einerlei, ob die Seele einem Weibe, einer Dichtung oder einem großen Werk und Plan zum Besten der Brüder des Erdentages gegeben werde. Nun war der Wald nur schön, erhaben, lieblich, feierlich: eine Seele hatte er nicht wiederzugeben, wie das Weib, wie die grau gefärbte Tafel, wie das arme Blatt weißen Papieres. Einsam blieb der Pfarrherr Friedemann Leutenbacher im Schatten wie im

The minister in Elend had in contrast to his times always maintained a most intimate intercourse with nature; indeed, the poor
man had no other refuge from his misery and the misery of his
surroundings than the forest. And if he knew little of the erudite
science of dismembering every beautiful living thing in the forest
and field and calling it by its Greek or Latin name, he nevertheless stuck to the names Adam had given things, and let them
affect him in each and every mood according to the way of
Adam. He saw the seasons of the year—he saw the mist, the rain,
the snow, the sunshine and moonlight come and go. He leaned
against the gnarled trunk of the oak in the shade and glanced
across the radiant land whose scenes of fire and carnage, whose
ravaged fields and meadows vanished and disappeared in the
universal beauty which man can never remove from this earth,
the stage on which he must act out his life. He lay during the
entire sunny day in the grass on the mountain slope, and glanced
out across the black letters of his New Testament into the mysterious gloom of his fir forest and heard the firs singing softly in
the breathing of the wind. Far and wide he was familiar with his
surroundings; he knew every rock and stone, every spring, every
clear-dark pool in the forest, and came to them to hold intercourse with them as with friends and relatives—today with this
one, tomorrow with that, however his heart and the anxious or
lighter mood of the day compelled. He composed a third of his
sermons in the forest; he bore his soul into the forest and gave his
soul to it.

But when a man gives his soul, he too must receive one in return, if the high blessing is not to be perverted into the bitterest
bane. And it is immaterial whether the soul be given to a woman,
a composition, or a great work and plan for the betterment of
one's fellowman in this earthly existence. The forest was merely
beautiful, lofty, pleasant, and solemn. It had no soul to reciprocate
like a woman, like the grey-colored slate, or like the poor sheet of
white paper. The minister, Friedemann Leutenbacher, remained
lonesome in the shadows as

Sonnenschein; selbst die Schönheit, Milde und Lieblichkeit der
Natur mußten erdrückend werden.

Seit langen Jahren wagte Friedemann nicht mehr, das Echo
mit seiner Stimme zu lustigem Gegenruf zu erwecken; er fürchtete sich vor der Stimme des Waldes, die seiner Verlassenheit
spottete. Oft fuhr er schaudernd zurück vor seinem Bild im
Quell oder im dunkeln, geheimnisvollen Waldteich; oft fuhr er
erschreckt zusammen, wenn plötzlich fern der Wind sich erhob,
über die Wipfel fuhr und sie mit dem Saum seines Gewandes
geisterhaft streifte. Dem Pfarrherrn von Wallrode fröstelte oft
in der heißesten Glut des Juli auf dem sonnigsten Wiesenflecke,
und der Duft, welchen der wolkenlose Sommermittag den Tannen und Fichten entlockte und der, wenn man nicht einsam ist,
berauschend wie junger Wein wirkt, füllte ihm Herz und Hirn
mit so jäher Angst und unsäglicher Beklemmung, daß er aus
dem Bereich desselben im Lauf entfliehen mußte, um dann,
atmend im freien Felde stehend, die pochenden Schläfen mit der
Hand zu drücken.

Weil dem Walde die Seele fehlte und weil Undine, die sich
nach einer Seele sehnte, nur ein schönes Märchen ist, konnte der
Pfarrherr von Wallrode im Elend nur den dritten Teil seiner
Predigten im Walde machen. Das erbarmungswürdige, halb tierische Leben um seine leere, halbzertrümmerte Behausung her
hatte doch wieder mehr dafür zu geben als die Natur. Als nun
von dem Frühling des Jahres sechzehnhundertsiebenunddreißig
an dem Walde eine Seele wuchs, da huben für den Pfarrer im
Elend das Wunder und der Zauber an.

Den Herbst und Winter des Jahres sechsunddreißig hindurch
hatte der Magister Konrad jeden Verkehr mit dem Pfarrherrn
schroff und mißtrauisch von sich gewiesen, und scheu, selber halb
furchtsam, hatte Ehrn Friedemann Leutenbacher, dessen Grüße
kaum erwidert wurden, die Gegend der hohen Tanne gemieden
und seine Schritte nach andern Richtungen gelenkt. Aber gegen
Ende des Frühlings siebenunddreißig trat eines Abends, als die
Sonne dem westlichen Horizont schon ziemlich nahe war, der

174

in the sunshine. Even the beauty, mildness, and charm of nature could only become oppressive.

For many years Friedemann had no longer dared to awaken the echo to a merry answering call; he feared the voice of the forest which mocked his aloneness. Frequently he recoiled shuddering from his image in the spring or in the dark and mysterious tarn. Often he gave a sudden start, when the wind unexpectedly stirred in the distance and blew over the tree tops, brushing them in a ghoulish fashion with the hem of its garments. The minister of Wallrode was often chilled in the extremest heat of July in the sunniest glade. And the fragrance which the cloudless summer noon enticed from the firs and pines, and which, if one is not lonely, has an intoxicating effect like new wine, filled his heart and brain with such a sudden anxiety and unspeakable oppression that he had to flee from its influence swiftly in order then to breathe standing in the open field, pressing his throbbing temples with his hands.

Because the forest had no soul, and because Undine, who longed for a soul, is only a pretty fable, the minister of Wallrode could compose only a third of his sermons in the forest. The pitiful, half animal-like life surrounding his empty, half-ruined dwelling had after all more to offer in return than nature. When in the spring of the year sixteen hundred and thirty-seven the forest received a soul, then began for the minister in Elend the magic and the enchantment.

Throughout the fall and winter of the year 'thirty-six, Master Conrad had rebuffed all intercourse with the pastor abruptly and distrustfully; and Friedemann Leutenbacher, whose greetings were hardly returned, had shyly, even half fearfully, avoided the region of the tall fir-tree, and turned his steps in other directions. But one evening toward the end of the spring of 'thirty-seven, when the sun was already approaching the western horizon,

fremde Mann dem Geistlichen jach in den Weg, grüßte ihn zum
ersten Male höflich, wenn auch finster, und fragte ihn, ob er
nicht eine Stelle wisse und kundgeben wolle, wo das Kräutlein
Hypericum, sonsten auch Sankt-Johannis-Kraut genannt, in
guter Menge wachse und zu finden sei. Er mußte seine Frage
eindringlicher wiederholen; denn so verwundert war der Pfarrherr über das plötzliche Entgegentreten aus dem Gebüsch und
das Anreden, daß er des Fremden Meinung zuerst ganz und gar
überhörte. Wohl aber wußte er, wo Gott ein jegliches heil-
kräftig, gesund, balsamisch oder giftig Kräutlein in seinem
Walde wachsen ließ—sei es in der Sonne, sei's im Schatten, sei's
am Felsgestein, sei's am Quell. Auch das Kraut Hypericum
kannte er nach Stand und Nutzen, schritt mit dem Magister zur
Stelle und half ihm pflücken. Da mußte zuletzt doch ein Wort
das andere geben und die beiden Männer aus ihrer gegenseitigen
Einsamkeit hinaus- und einander entgegenführen. Der Pfarrherr
erfuhr, daß das kleine Mädchen seit dem harten Winter in der
Hütte krank liege und sich trotz des neuen Frühlings und der
schönern Tage nicht wieder erholen und zurechtwerden könne.
Der Fremde erfuhr, daß Ehrn Friedemann Leutenbacher ein
Mann sei, mit welchem sich wohl in jeder Sache ein gut Wort
reden und ein guter Rat halten lasse. So waren die beiden, ihnen
selber fast unvermerkt, nahe an die Hütte gekommen, und es
mußte geschehen, daß der Magister Konrad den Pfarrherrn ein-
lud, einzutreten unter das Dach, so er hatte aufrichten helfen,
und das kranke Mägdlein anzusehen. Zum ersten Male stand
der Pfarrherr in dem Raume, vor dessen Gerät und Bewohnern
dem Dorfe Wallrode so sehr grauete. Er sah die Bücher und
wenigen mathematischen und physikalischen Instrumente, und
er sah die kleine, kranke Else, die mit großen, dunkelblauen,
fieberkranken Augen ihn von ihrem Lager aus anblickte und,
nachdem sie seine Gestalt und Miene erkundet hatte, lächelte
und ihn lieblich nickend grüßte. Die Bücher und Instrumente
zogen den Pfarrherrn von Wallrode wohl recht an, gleich alten,
trefflichen, lang entbehrten Bekannten aus längst vergangener

the stranger stepped suddenly into the path of the minister and greeted him courteously for the first time, if somewhat somberly. He asked the pastor whether he knew of a place, and would inform him, where one could find the herb *hypericum*, otherwise known as St. John's wort, growing in abundance. He had to repeat the question more pointedly, for the pastor was so surprised at this sudden appearance from the bushes and the request that at first he failed entirely to grasp the meaning of the stranger's words. But yes, he did know where God let each healing, healthful, and soothing or poisonous herb grow in His forest, whether in the shade or sun, whether under the rock at the cliff or at the spring, he also knew the habitat and use of the herb *hypericum*. He accompanied the teacher to the proper place and helped him pluck it. One word naturally led to another, coaxing both men out of their mutual loneliness toward one another. The pastor learned that the little girl had lain sick in the hut since the hard winter, and was unable to recover and become normal again despite the arrival of spring and the pleasanter days. The stranger learned that Friedemann Leutenbacher was a man with whom one might converse well on any subject and with whom one would do well to hold counsel. Thus, both had almost unwittingly arrived at the hut, and it was inevitable that Master Conrad would invite the pastor to see the maiden who lay sick under the roof which he had helped erect. For the first time the pastor stood in the room whose furnishings and inhabitants the villagers of Wallrode dreaded so much. He saw the books and few mathematical and physical instruments; he saw the sick little Else, who gazed at him from her couch with large, dark blue, fever-sick eyes. After recognizing his figure and features, she smiled and greeted him pleasantly with a nod. The books and instruments naturally attracted the curate of Wallrode like old, excellent, long-lost acquaintances of a time long past;

Zeit; aber mit noch größerer Wehmut und Rührung würde er
sie gegrüßt haben, wenn des Mägdleins Augen es gelitten hätten. Dem Zauber, der aus diesen beiden dunkeln Kindesaugen
auf den Mann, den Diener am Worte Gottes, den Gelehrten,
den Menschen, der so viel litt und erfuhr, strahlte, war nicht zu
widerstehen;—von dieser Stunde, von diesem Augenblick an
war Friedemann Leutenbacher an die Hütte des Magisters Konradus gebannt; von diesem Augenblicke an bekam der große
Wald eine Seele, und der Pfarrherr brauchte nicht mehr aus ihm
zu fliehen, weil er sich fürchtete in seiner Einsamkeit. Dieses
Kind bedeutete für den Mann aus dem Elend die Offenbarung
eines Daseins, welches er nicht kannte, nach welchem er nur ein
dumpfes, schmerzvolles, unbestimmtes Sehnen im Herzen trug.
Dieses Kind wußte nichts von der grausen Last, die auf der
Erde und dem Herzen des Pfarrers von Wallrode im Elend lag.—
    Noch längere Zeit, nachdem die Tochter leicht und heiter dem
Geistlichen entgegengegangen war, blieb der Meister Konrad
verschlossen und finster und gestattete erst allmählich, als der
Einfluß des Gelehrten auf den Gelehrten zu wirken begonnen
hatte, einen tiefern Einblick in die Geschichte seines Lebens. Das
Unglück maß damals mit einem gewaltigen Maß, und kein
Schrecken und Schmerz, welche den Menschen treffen mochten,
waren so groß, daß sie nicht noch durch gräßlicheres Unheil
überboten werden konnten. Seinen Namen nannte der Magister
nie; doch von seinen Schicksalen erzählte er im Laufe der Jahre
bruchstücksweise, und das Herz erzitterte, sie zu hören; wir
können aber nur kurz davon Bericht geben, da wir nicht seine
Geschichte beschreiben.
    Er war ein Lehrer an der Domschule der unglücklichen Stadt
Magdeburg gewesen, und mit seinem Hause waren sein Weib
und seine beiden ältesten Kinder verbrannt am zehnten Mai des
Jahres sechzehnhunderteinunddreißig. Ihn selber hatte das Geschick mit dem jüngsten Kind in die Domkirche unter die tausend jammervollen Menschen geschleudert, welchen nach drei
Tagen der Todesangst der kaiserliche General Johann Tzerklas

176

but with still greater sadness and sympathy would he have greeted them, had the maiden's eyes permitted it. The magic which shone from those two dark childish eyes on the man, the minister of the word of God, the scholar, the human being who had suffered so much and experienced so much, was not to be resisted. From this hour, from this moment Friedemann Leutenbacher was bound by a spell to the hut of Master Conrad. From this moment on, the great forest received a soul, and the pastor needed no longer to fly from it because he was afraid in his loneliness. This child symbolized for the man of Elend the revelation of an existence that he did not know, but for which he had been carrying in his heart only a dull, painful, and indefinite longing. This child knew nothing of the hideous burden which weighed upon the earth and upon the heart of the minister of Wallrode in Elend.

For a considerable time after his daughter had approached the clergyman freely and cheerfully, Master Conrad remained reticent and gloomy; and only as the influence of scholar upon scholar began to have its effect, did he gradually grant the minister a deeper insight into the story of his life. Misfortune measured in those days with a mighty measure, and no terror or pain that might come to a man was so great that it could not be outdone by some more horrible misfortune. The scholar never mentioned his name; yet he told something of his fate in the course of years bit by bit, and the heart trembles at hearing it. We can, however, give only a short report of it, since we are not describing his history.

He had been a teacher at the cathedral school of the unfortunate city of Magdeburg, and when his house was burned on the tenth of May sixteen hundred and thirty, his wife and both his elder children lost their lives. Moreover, fate had thrown him with his youngest child into the cathedral among the thousand miserable human beings to whom the imperial general, John Tzerklas

von Tilly das schenkte, was allein er ihnen nicht nahm, das
Leben. Des Meisters Name stand auch unter dem Briefe, in welchem die letzten übriggebliebenen Bewohner der großen zer-
trümmerten Stadt die stromabwärts liegenden Städte, Dörfer
und Flecken bis nach Hamburg um Gottes und Jesu Christi willen baten, die sechstausend Leichname ihrer Mitbürger und Verwandten, welche der Feind, um die Gassen zu räumen, in die
Elbe geworfen hatte, nicht den Tieren des Waldes und Feldes
zu überlassen, sondern sie barmherzig und christlich zu bestat-
ten, wenn der Fluß sie zu ihnen tragen würde. Vier Jahre
wohnte der Magister Konrad unter den Trümmern. Auf die
erste stumpfsinnige Betäubung folgte die gottlästernde Ver-
zweiflung und dieser die unheilbare, herzzerfressende, täglich
wachsende Melancholie. Das neue Leben, welches sich auf der
schwarzgebrannten, blutgetränkten Stätte um ihn her kümmerlich und kläglich erhob, hatte keinen Sinn für ihn; die Geister
der erschlagenen dreißigtausend Männer, Weiber und Kinder,
welche in den Ruinen umgingen, machten diese winzige, trost-
lose Lebendigkeit selber zu einem Spuk, und der Schatten der
versunkenen Stadt duldete kein Sonnenlicht über den neuen
Wohnstätten, die aus rauchgeschwärzten Mauersteinen und
halbverkohlten Balken langsam aufwuchsen. Und die Pest saß
mit unter den Trümmern und wich nicht; neue Kriegsstürme
brausten heran und drangen durch die alten Breschen der Wallonen und Kroaten und fuhren grimmig durch die offenen Pforten der Stadt, deren Torflügel seit dem zehnten Mai zu Boden
lagen wie alles andere. Vergeblich versuchte es der Gelehrte, seinen Lehrstuhl wiederaufzurichten; in allem vernichtet, wich der
Meister Konrad im vierten Jahre nach der Verwüstung gen
Halberstadt und von dort in den Wald, um den Menschen, dem
Greuel der Welt ganz zu entfliehen und sein Kind zu retten aus
dem Chaos und der Sünde der Zeit.—Wir haben erzählt, wie
ihm die Leute von Wallrode im Elend und ihr Pfarrer Friedemann Leutenbacher seine Hütte an der hohen Tanne bauen halfen und wie er sein Einsiedlerleben daselbst begann.———

von Tilly, after three days of mortal anxiety, granted their lives
—the one thing he had not taken from them. The name of the
scholar stood also below the letter signed by the last remaining
inhabitants of the great ruined city to the villages and hamlets lying downstream as far as Hamburg. It implored them in the name
of the Lord and our Saviour not to abandon to the beasts of the
forest and field the six thousand corpses of their relatives and
fellow citizens which the enemy had thrown into the Elbe to
clear the streets, but to give them a merciful and Christian burial,
should the river carry them so far. For four years Master Conrad
dwelt among the ruins. The first deadening stupefaction was
followed by impious despair and after that an incurable, heart-
consuming, daily increasing melancholy. The new life which
arose pitiably and wretchedly from the fire-charred and blood-
drenched place around him had no meaning for Master Conrad.
The spirits of the thirty thousand slaughtered men, women, and
children which haunted the ruins made of this poor comfortless
life itself a phantom; and the shadow of the fallen city suffered no
sunlight to shine over the new dwellings which gradually arose
out of smoke-blackened bricks and charred beams, and the plague
sat among the ruins and would not yield. New war storms roared
on and penetrated through the old breaches made by the Walloons and Croats, raging fiercely through the open city-gates
whose wings had been torn off and had been, like everything else,
lying on the ground since the tenth of May. In vain the scholar
attempted to begin his teaching again; frustrated in everything,
Master Conrad withdrew in the fourth year after the devastation
to Halberstadt, and from there into the forest in order to escape
mankind and the horrors of the world entirely and to save his
child from the chaos and sinfulness of the time. We have related
how the populace of Wallrode in Elend and their minister Friède-
mann Leutenbacher helped him to build his hut under the tall fir-
tree and how he began his hermit's existence there.

Wollte dieser Schneesturm nimmer zu einem Ende kommen?
Mächtiger und mächtiger sauste und brauste es und schüttete die
weißen Lasten auf Forst und Dorf. Es knackte und knirschte
das Gezweig, es krachten die Stämme; der Wolf heulte, wenn
die Windsbraut Atem schöpfte, und durch all den Aufruhr der
Natur klang dem Pfarrer Friedemann Leutenbacher ein Lied
ins Ohr, Verse aus einem Liede, welches Else von der Tanne gesungen hatte:

> „Vierzehn lange, lange Wochen
> Gab die Liga Sturm auf Sturm,
> Vierzehn lange, lange Wochen
> Trotzte Mauer, Wall und Turm.
> Tapfre, fromme, teutsche Bürger
> Schützten Glauben, Ehr und Haus,—
> Dreißigtausend Ketzerleben
> Rottet heut die Kirche aus!
>
> Stadt gewonnen! all gewonnen!
> Und des Kaisers Feldherr spricht:
> Seit Jerusalem verloren,
> Sah man solch Viktori nicht!
> Heilige Jungfrau, Mutter Gottes,
> Dank und Gloria! Dir die Ehr!
> Seit man Troja hat gewonnen,
> Sah man solchen Sieg nicht mehr!“

Aber nicht bloß dieses Lied, nein manch andere Weisen, deren
Noten niemals eine Menschenhand auf Papier festgebannt hatte
wie die Buchstaben eines Buches, sang Else von der Tanne! Else
von der Tanne, die schönste Maid—Else von der Tanne, die von
der Sünde und dem Greuel der Welt im Wald, im Elend un-
berührt geblieben war! Else von der Tanne, die reinste, heiligste
Blume in der grauenvollen Wüstenei der Erde—Else von der
Tanne, die Seele des großen Waldes! Der Pfarrer Friedemann
Leutenbacher im Elend mußte beide Hände vor das Gesicht

Would this snow storm never come to an end? More and more violently it blustered and roared and shook its white burdens upon forest and village. The branches crackled and creaked; the tree-trunks groaned. The wolf howled whenever the gale caught its breath, and amid all the tumult of nature a song sounded in the ears of Friedemann Leutenbacher, verses of a song that Else von der Tanne had sung:

> "Fourteen weeks of endless fighting
> Storm'd the League against our pow'r,
> Fourteen weeks of endless fighting
> Storm'd against the wall and tow'r.
> Brave and pious German burghers
> Fought for honor, faith, and home.
> Heretics to thirty thousand
> Slays today the church of Rome.
>
> City taken! All is taken!
> And the Kaiser's Marshal said:
> Since Jerusalem has fallen
> Was no equal triumph made.
> Holy Virgin! Heavenly Mother!
> Grace and glory! Praise to thee.
> Since the city Troy was taken
> Ne'er was such a victory!"

But not merely this song—no, many another melody whose notes no human hand had ever fixed like the letter of a book on paper Else von der Tanne had been wont to sing. Else von der Tanne, the comeliest maiden—Else von der Tanne, who had remained untouched by the sin and horror of the world in the forest in Elend! Else von der Tanne, the purest, holiest flower in this dismal wilderness of the earth—Else von der Tanne, the soul of the great forest. The minister in Elend, Friedemann Leutenbacher, could not help pressing both hands to his face;

schlagen, er mußte bitter weinen: die winterliche Sturmnacht
mußte endlich doch zu ihrem Ende gelangen; aber *die* Nacht,
welche sein Leben jetzt bedrohte, *die* konnte nicht enden, solange er noch unter den Lebenden wandelte.

Else von der Tanne hatte als Kind an seiner Seite gesessen und
hatte um seine Kniee gespielt, während er mit ihrem finstern
Vater ernstes Gespräch über der Welt Lauf und Bedrängnis
pflog. Er war so jung geblieben in seiner Verlassenheit, daß er
mit ihr ein Kind sein konnte, daß in ihrem kindischen Herzen
kein Ton anklingen konnte, der nicht in seiner Brust einen
Widerhall fand. Gleich einem Träumenden kam er stets von
einem solchen lieblichen Verkehr heim in seine öde Wohnung,
zu seinem armen, blöden, gequälten, mißtrauischen Volk. Es
war ein ander Ding, mit dem kleinen Mädchen am Weiher mitten im dunkeln Forst zu sitzen als allein mit der Furcht vor dem
eigenen Bild im Wasser. Das lachende Gesichtchen des Kindes
in der Flut war nicht gespenstisch. An der Seite Elses schauderte
und fröstelte den Pfarrherrn nicht mehr vor den hohen Geheimnissen der Natur;—Else von der Tanne verstand die Sprache
der Tiere, des Windes, des Lichtes ganz anders und viel besser
als der Pfarrherr, und der Pfarrherr hatte viel mehr von dem
Kinde zu lernen als das Kind von ihm.

Wie sich die junge Seele von Frühling zu Frühling mehr ent-
faltete, erschlossen sich auch mehr und höhere Geheimnisse in
der Brust Friedemann Leutenbachers, und als Else von der
Tanne die schönste der Jungfrauen geworden war, da war der
Pfarrer im Elend mit ihr gewachsen und trotz seiner Jahre so
jung wie sie. Es war entsetzlich—ein Schmerz sondergleichen,
an diesen Glanz, diese Holdseligkeit des Lebens, welche auf
ewig versinken sollten, in dieser winterlichen Sturmesnacht den-
ken zu müssen.

Gestern noch war der Wald grün, gestern noch blühten alle
Blumen, sprangen alle Quellen; gestern noch wandelte Else von
der Tanne in der Anmutigkeit des Jahres, und so weit auch
Friedemann Leutenbacher vom höchsten Bergesgipfel über die

he could not help weeping bitterly. The stormy winter night would doubtless come to an end, but the night that threatened his life now could not end as long as he walked upon the earth.

Else von der Tanne had as a child sat at his side and had played at his feet, while he engaged her melancholy father in earnest conversation concerning the course of the world and its tribulations. He had remained so young in his solitude that he could be a child with her—that no note could be struck in her childish heart that did not find an echo in his own breast. Like one in a dream he always returned home from such pleasant intercourse to his desolate dwelling, to his poor, stupid, tortured, and distrustful people. Sitting with the little maid beside the pond in the midst of the dark forest was quite a different thing from being alone with the fear of his own image in the water. The small laughing face of the child on the water was at least not ghostly; at Else's side the deep secrets of nature no longer caused the pastor to shudder and grow chill. Else von der Tanne understood the language of the animals, the wind, and the light quite differently from, and much better than, the pastor; and the pastor had much more to learn from the child than the child from him.

As the young soul developed more and more from spring to spring, more and more and greater and greater secrets enclosed themselves in the breast of Friedemann Leutenbacher. And when Else von der Tanne had become the most beautiful of maidens, the minister of Elend had grown with her, and despite his years was as young as she. It was terrible—a pain without equal on this stormy winter's night to have to think of this splendor and loveliness of life which were destined to vanish forever.

Only yesterday the forest was still green; only yesterday the flowers were all still blooming, and all the springs were bubbling; only yesterday Else von der Tanne was walking in all the charm of the year, and however far Friedemann Leutenbacher might gaze from the highest mountain top across the

Herrlichkeit des blühenden, funkelnden Landes blicken mochte,
nichts Herrlicheres gab es, so weit das Auge und das Herz reich-
ten, als Else von der Tanne.

Die schwarzen, schrecklichen Striche, welche die Heereszüge
durch die Ebene gezogen hatten, waren ausgelöscht; die roten
Narben um die Handgelenke des Pfarrherrn von Wallrode
waren Zeichen der Verheißung, wie der Griff des Engels an der
Hüfte Jakobs auf der Stätte Pnuel, die da heißt: Ich habe Gott
gesehen, und meine Seele ist genesen.

Gestern, gestern! Wer kann den Gram ermessen, welcher sich
in dem kleinen Worte bergen kann? Es ist der gierige Schlund,
der das gespenstische Morgen gebiert, welches uns mit tausendfachen Schrecken ängstet, bis die finstere Höhle, die alles ver-
schlingt, wodurch wir leben, uns selber in ihre Tiefen herab-
zieht.

Gestern wandelte Else von der Tanne im Lichte des Frühlings
und des Lebens, und heute—heute schrieb der Pfarrherr zu
Wallrode im Elend die Weihnachtspredigt für sein Dorf, durch
welches Else von der Tanne getötet worden war.

Dies aber ist die Geschichte des Todes der Jungfrau.

In der fünften Woche nach Pfingsten des Jahres sechzehnhundertachtundvierzig, am Tage Johannis des Täufers, wollte
Ehrn Friedemann Leutenbacher in seinem verwüsteten Kirch-
lein das Abendmahl austeilen, und am Tage vorher hatte ihm
der Meister Konrad im Walde gesagt, daß er mit seinem Kinde
herniedersteigen würde, um des heiligen Geheimnisses teilhaftig
zu werden. Else aber hatte zu diesen Worten ihres Vaters genickt und lächelnd gesprochen:

„Ja, Herr Pfarrer, wir kommen herab aus dem Walde; und
dann nehmen wir Euch nach dem heiligen Werke mit uns zurück. Es ist mein Geburtstag morgen, den müsset Ihr mir feiern
helfen. Ihr müsset mir ein Sträußlein und einen Glückwunsch in
Reimen bringen."

Ehrn Friedemann hatte auch gelächelt und genickt und gesagt, er wolle schauen, daß er die Blumen zum Strauß und die

splendor of the sparkling land in bloom, there was nothing more splendid, as far as the eye and heart could reach, than Else von der Tanne.

The black horrible marks which the marching armies had left on the plain were obliterated. The red scars about the wrists of the pastor of Wallrode were symbols of a covenant like the touch of the angel on the hollow of Jacob's thigh at the place called Peniel, which is written: I have seen God face to face and my soul is preserved.

Yesterday! Yesterday! Who can fathom the grief which can hide in that little word? It is the greedy chasm, begetter of the ghostly "tomorrow," which plagues us with a thousand terrors until that murky abyss which swallows up everything whereby we live draws us too into its depths.

Yesterday Else von der Tanne was walking in the light of spring and of life, and today—today the pastor of Wallrode in Elend was writing the Christmas sermon for his village, which had killed Else von der Tanne.

But here is the story of the maiden's death. In the fifth week after Whitsunday of the year sixteen hundred and forty-eight on the day of St. John the Baptist, the Reverend Friedemann Leutenbacher was to administer the Lord's Supper in his desolated church, and on the previous day Master Conrad had told him in the forest that he would come down with his child to partake of the holy mystery. Else had nodded at these words of her father, and said, smiling:

"Yes, Reverend, we shall come down from the forest and then we shall take you back with us after the worship service. Tomorrow is my birthday. You must help me celebrate it; you must bring me a little bouquet and congratulations in verse."

The Reverend Friedemann Leutenbacher had also smiled and nodded, saying he would find flowers for the bouquet and

Reime zum guten Wunsch mit den Blumen am Wege zum Walde
finde.

Dann hatte er, als der Mond aufstieg, Abschied genommen
und hatte, als er sich am Fels wendete, die zarte Gestalt im weißen Schein des Mondes stehen sehen und neben ihr das zahme
Reh. Die letzte Nachtigall des Jahres hatte ihr letztes Lied gesungen, und als der Pfarrer aus dem Walde hervorgetreten war,
lag über den Bergen jenseits des Dorfes ein fernes Gewitter, dessen Blitze er leuchten sah, dessen Donner er aber nicht hören
konnte. Die ganze Nacht hindurch war er von bösen, angstvollen Träumen geplagt; und wenn er sich halb ermunterte,
nachdem er erschreckt aus dem peinlichen Schattenspiel aufge-
fahren war, vermeinte er immerfort den heftigsten Regen auf
seinem morschen Dach und vor seinem Fenster zu vernehmen.
Das war jedoch nur Täuschung; nur ein nicht starker Wind
rauschte die halbe Nacht, von Mitternacht an, in den Bäumen,
und die aufsteigende frühe Sonne fand einen wolkenfreien Himmel, ihre Bahn daran durch einen schönen Sommertag zu laufen.

Die kleine Kirchenglocke hatten die Kroaten mit sich fortge-
führt; sie konnte die Gemeinde nicht zusammenrufen. Ein Kind,
vom Pfarrhaus geschickt, lief von Hütte zu Hütte und sagte an,
daß der Pastor zum Dienste am Worte Gottes bereit sei.

Mit Sonnenaufgang hatten der Magister Konrad und Else
ihre Hütte verlassen, ohne von dem Dorfkinde aufgefordert zu
sein. Lieblich lag der Sonnenmorgen über dem Walde; lieblich
erregten sich die Vögel in Baum, Strauch und blauer Luft; und
jeder Quell sprang und lief freudiger und mutwilliger in den
Johannistag hinein.

Das zahme Reh begleitete die schöne Herrin mit fröhlichen
Sprüngen und schmeichelndem Anschmiegen durch den Forst;
und der Meister und Vater mit seinem jetzt so weißen ehrwür-
digen Bart und seinem langen Stabe glich wahrlich wohl einem
Zauberer, aber einem guten, der ein aus dem Bann und der Gewalt unheimlicher Mächte gerettetes Königskind durch den Forst
geleitete.

rhymes for felicitations with the flowers on the way to the forest.

Then as the moon rose, he had taken his departure and had, as he turned around by the cliff, seen her delicate figure standing in the light of the moon and beside her the tame roe. The last nightingale of the year had sung its last song; and when the minister stepped out of the forest, a violent thunder storm was raging in the mountains beyond the village; its lightning he saw flashing, but its thunder he could not hear. Throughout the night he was plagued by evil and fearful dreams and when, after having started up out of the painful phantasmagoria, he was half awake, he kept imagining that he heard a most heavy rain on his decaying roof and in front of his window. But that was only an illusion. Only a mild wind soughed in the trees half the night, from midnight on; and the early rising sun found a cloudless sky in which to run its course throughout a pretty summer's day.

The Croats had carried off the small church bell with them; it could no longer call together the congregation. A child, sent from the parsonage, ran from hut to hut, announcing that the pastor was ready for the holy service.

Master Conrad and Else had left their hut at sunrise without being notified by the child from the village. Pleasant lay the summer's morning over the forest; pleasantly the birds flitted in tree, bush, and blue air; and every spring was welling and running more joyfully and wantonly to greet the day of St. John.

The tame roe accompanied its pretty mistress with joyous leaps and coaxing nudges through the forest; and the scholar and father with his now so very white and venerable beard and his long staff was truly like a magician, but a good one, who was conducting through the forest a princess rescued from the spell and power of sinister forces.

Bis an den Rand des großen Waldes ging das Reh freudig mit der Herrin, wie im Tanz; doch als ein letzter lustiger Sprung unter den letzten Bäumen es plötzlich in das helle Sonnenlicht brachte, da fuhr es im jähen Schreck zusammen und zurück. Zitternd stand's und sah nach dem Dorf hinunter, und dann gebärdete es sich ganz seltsam und wollte in keiner Weise leiden, daß die Jungfrau fürderschreite und den grünen Schatten verlasse. Trotz aller Liebkosungen und Beschwichtigungen wurde es immer heftiger und ungebärdiger, so daß es zuletzt vom Meister Konrad schier mit Gewalt verscheucht werden mußte. Ach, es redete nur seine Sprache, und die konnten oder wollten die stolzen Menschen nicht verstehen. Betrübt stand es unter den Bäumen und sah dem Meister und der schönen Else nach, wie sie auf dem gewundenen Wege durch die kümmerlich bestellten Felder gegen das Dorf schritten; dann stürzte es im wildesten Lauf durch den Wald und verlor sich im Dickicht, wie gejagt von Angst und Entsetzen.

Schon auf dem Feldwege trafen der Vater und die Tochter mit Leuten zusammen, die ihren Gruß nicht erwiderten, auf freundliche Worte nicht antworteten, sondern sich scheu und mißtrauisch abwendeten und zur Seite weiterschlichen. Deren Blicke und Gebärden warnten deutlicher, als die Augen des Rehes es vermochten; aber die Wanderer ließen sich auch durch sie nicht den Weg versperren, sondern wanderten langsam fürbaß, ein jedes tief versunken in seine eigenen Gedanken, ihrem Ziele zu.

An dem Kirchweg saß ein altes Weiblein, dessen Ruf im Dorfe auch bös war wegen teuflischen Willens und Vermögens, dessen Macht aber zu sehr gefürchtet wurde, als daß man sich an ihm vergriffen hätte. Diese alte Frau hob, als die Jungfrau vorüberschritt, das Haupt von den Knieen, winkte mit der dürren Hand und rief mit heiserer Stimme:

„Hüt dich, hüt dich, Mägdlein! Hüt dein jung Leben, Liebchen! Dein Schatten gehet vor dir, fall nicht über deinen Schatten! Wer fällt, fällt in seinen Schatten, und nicht alle stehen wieder auf."

The roe accompanied its mistress joyfully up to the edge of the great forest, dancing all the while; but when its last merry leap among the last trees brought it suddenly into the bright sunlight, it recoiled in a sudden fright. Trembling, it stood looking down at the village and then, acting most strangely, it would in no way suffer the maiden to step farther and leave the shade of the green trees. In spite of all stroking and hushing it became more and more violent and unruly, so that it had finally to be frightened off by Master Conrad with sheer force. Alas, it spoke only its own language, and proud men could not, or would not, understand it. Downcast, it stood under the trees gazing after the scholar and the beautiful Else as they proceeded toward the village on the winding path through the miserably husbanded fields. Then it vaulted in the wildest career through the forest and disappeared in the thicket, as if chased by dread and horror.

Even on the road across the fields the father and daughter encountered people who did not return their greetings or answer their friendly words, but turned aside nervously and distrustfully, and shied farther to the side. Their looks and actions were more understandable warnings that the eyes of the roe. But the wanderers were undeterred by them, and continued slowly toward their goal, each sunk deep in his own thoughts.

By the side of the church road sat a little old woman whose reputation in the village was also bad on account of her diabolical powers and intentions, yet whose power was too greatly feared for anyone to lay hands on her. This old woman raised her head from her knees as the maiden passed by, beckoned with her withered hand, and cried in a hoarse voice,

"Careful, careful, little girl! Be careful for your young life, my dear. Your shadow goes in front of you; don't fall over your shadow. He who falls, falls in his shadow, and not all get up again."

Der Meister Konrad schüttelte nur traurig den Kopf, doch
Else von der Tanne nickte dankbar;—mit heiserer Stimme sang
die Alte hinter ihr:

„Herzeleins pochend Weben
Kündet dir: Tod im Leben!—
Stirn so weiß und fein,
Denk: Schatten im Sonnenschein!"

Dann legte sie das Gesicht wieder auf die Kniee.—
Auf dem Friedhofe vor der Kirche wartete die Gemeinde von
Wallrode im Elend ihres Predigers. Die Alten schwatzten unter-
einander, die Jungen kosten und lachten oder neckten und höhn-
ten einander, die Kinder jagten sich um die Gräber; aber als der
Meister Konrad und Else sich zeigten, kam das alles zu einem
plötzlichen Ende, und eine solche Bewegung entstand unter dem
Volk, daß die Jungfrau jetzt fast ebenso angstvoll wie ihr Reh-
lein sich an den Vater drängte und dieser unwillkürlich seinen
Stab zur Abwehr fester faßte.

„Die Hex! die Hex! der Hexenmeister!" ging es anfangs leise,
dann immer lauter in der Runde. „Was wollen sie hier? weshalb
kommen sie herab aus ihrem Schlupfloch? Sie sollen bleiben, wo
sie sind! sie sollen nicht herniederkommen ins Dorf! Schlagt sie
—treibet sie von dannen—räuchert sie aus!"

Als der Pfarrer Friedemann Leutenbacher in diesem Augenblick auf dem Kirchhofe erschien, wurde auch er bedenklich an-
gesehen und von den erregten Pfarrkindern bedrohlich ange-
gangen, den beiden Fremden den Kirchhof und die Kirche zu
verbieten. Kaum vermochte sein heiliges Amt, sein schwarz Pre-
digergewand und die erhobene Bibel seinen zürnenden Gegen-
worten Folge und Gehorsam zu schaffen und dem Magister
Konradus sowie der schönen Tochter einen freien Weg zu der
Tür des Gotteshauses zu bahnen. Als er sogar die Hand der
Jungfrau faßte, sie die zertretenen Stufen hinaufzuführen, da
ballte sein Dorf die Fäuste und schrie auf, als müsse nun der
blaue Himmel herabstürzen.

183

Master Conrad only shook his head sadly, but Else von der Tanne nodded gratefully. The old woman sang in a hoarse voice after her,

> "Little heart's throbbing weaving
> Foretells: Death in living!
> Brow so white and fine;
> Think: Shadow in sunshine!"

Then she laid her face on her knees again.

At the graveyard in front of the church the congregation of Wallrode in Elend were waiting for their preacher. The old people were gossiping among themselves; the boys were chattering and laughing, or teasing and mocking one another; the children were romping among the graves. But when Master Conrad and Else appeared, all that came abruptly to an end, and such a commotion arose among the people that the maiden now pressed against her father almost as anxiously as her little roe, as he involuntarily grasped his staff more firmly for defense.

"The witch! The witch! The sorcerer!" it went the rounds softly at first, then louder and louder. "What do they want here? Why are they coming down here out of their hiding-place? They ought to stay where they are! They should not come down here to the village. Hit them, drive them away, smoke them out!"

When the minister, Friedemann Leutenbacher, appeared at this moment in the churchyard, he himself was looked at askance and was approached threateningly by the aroused parishioners, who intended to prevent the two strangers from entering the churchyard and the church. His holy office, his black ministerial gown, and his upraised Bible were hardly able to procure compliance and obedience to his angry commands or to force a way open to the door of the church for Master Conrad and his pretty daughter. Even as he grasped the hand of the maiden to lead her up the worn steps, everyone in the village balled his fist and yelled out as if the blue sky would actually crash down.

Aber der Pfarrer zu Wallrode im Elend sah und hörte nicht;
mit erklingendem Herzen führte er Else von der Tanne in sein
Gotteshaus und bestieg gleich einem Schlafwandler die nach der
letzten Zerstörung roh wiederaufgerichtete Kanzel.

Ihm nach drängte sich der größere Teil der Gemeinde in die
Kirche und füllte den Raum mit Gemurr und Gemurmel.—

Grünes Gezweig rankte sich durch den verkohlten Dachstuhl,
durch die scheibenlosen Fenster und die Mauerrisse. Mit dem
Grün, der Sonne und der Luft war auch das flatternde, sum-
mende, zwitschernde Leben eingedrungen;—lieblich und glänzend
war der Tag, lieblich und glänzend war das Gesicht Elses unter
der Kanzel, und der Pfarrer Friedemann Leutenbacher sah nicht
die Gesichter seiner Gemeinde. Ihm war zumute, als sei er im
Wald, mitten im sichern, sonnigen, beseelten Walde, und habe
nur Else von der Tanne, um zu ihr zu reden. So begann er seine
Johannispredigt und wußte nicht, was zu derselben Zeit vor
der Tür der Kirche vorging.

Da war ein junges Weib zu einem frischen Grabe gesprungen,
hatte drei Hände voll Erde davon aufgegriffen und sie auf die
Schwelle der Kirchentür gestreut. Ein wüster, wildblickender
Bub von zwanzig Jahren war nach der Linde vor dem verbrannten Gemeindehause gelaufen und hatte von dem Baum,
an welchem im Jahre vierundvierzig Hatzfelds Kürassiere den
Ortsvorsteher aufhängten, einen dürren Zweig gebrochen. In
atemlosem Laufe kam er mit demselben zurück und warf ihn
auf die Schwelle der Sakristeitür. Nun waren die Hexe und der
Zaubermeister in dem Gotteshause gebannt;—solange die Erde
von dem neuen Grabe und der Ast vom Baume des Gehängten
auf den beiden Schwellen lagen, konnte kein unheiliger Fuß sie
überschreiten.

In herzklopfender Erwartung lauerten die auf dem Friedhofe zurückgebliebenen Leute aus Wallrode im Elend auf das,
was nun geschehen werde, jetzt, da der eine Zauber durch den
andern Zauber gebrochen und zunichte gemacht worden war. In
dem Sonnenschein auf und zwischen den Gräbern saßen und

But the minister of Wallrode in Elend neither saw nor heard; with a throbbing heart he led Else von der Tanne into his church and like one walking in his sleep he mounted the pulpit which had been roughly erected again after the last destruction.

Most of the congregation pressed after him into the church and filled the room with muttering and murmuring.

Green vines had sent their tendrils through the charred rafters of the roof, through the paneless windows and the crannies in the wall. Along with all this green life, with the air and sunshine, that fluttering, zooming, twittering life had also found its way in. Pleasant and radiant was the day—pleasant and radiant was the countenance of Else below the pulpit. The minister, Friedemann Leutenbacher, did not see the faces of his parishioners; he felt as if he were in the midst of the secure, sunny, soul-endowed forest, talking only to Else von der Tanne. Thus he began his sermon on the day of St. John, without knowing what was taking place at the same time in front of the church door.

There a young woman had jumped onto a fresh grave, picked up three handfuls of earth from it and scattered them upon the threshold of the church door. A dishevelled, wild-looking boy of twenty had run to the linden-tree in front of the burned townhall and had broken a dry branch from the tree on which the village magistrate had been hanged by Hatzfeld's cuirassiers in the year 'forty-four. Running breathlessly, he came back with it, and threw it upon the threshold of the sacristy door. Now the witch and sorcerer were put under a magic spell in the church; as long as the earth of the new grave and the branch from the gallows-tree lay upon the two thresholds no unholy foot was able to step over them.

Now that the one spell had been counteracted by the other and rendered harmless, the people of Wallrode in Elend that had been left behind in the graveyard awaited in heart-throbbing expectancy what was to happen next. They were standing and sitting in the sunshine among the graves,

standen sie, starr die beiden Pforten im Auge haltend, selber
bösen, schadenfrohen, heimtückischen Geistern und Kobolden
so ähnlich als möglich. Gierig warteten sie auf das Ende des
Gottesdienstes.

In der Kirche gab der Prediger Friedemann Leutenbacher den
Leib, der für die Welt gebrochen, und das Blut, das für sie ver-
gossen wurde;—alle, die auch ihr Teil Schuld an Elses Tode
trugen, tranken aus dem Becher, welchen die Lippen der Jungfrau berührt hatten.

Als der Pfarrer das schlechte Zinngefäß dem süßen Munde
der Jungfrau darbot, durchrieselte ihn ein heiliger Schauer, ein
Gefühl unendlichen Glückes. Es war Friede in seiner Seele wie
auf der Erde; sein Leben war nicht in die Zeit des fürchterlich-
sten aller Kriege gefallen; in eine einzige Minute fiel die Wonne
eines ganzen Daseins, und als dieser Augenblick vorübergegan-
gen war, hatte Friedemann Leutenbacher auf Erden nichts mehr
zu erwarten.

Mit einem dumpfen, verworrenen Lärm stürzte seine Gemeinde aus der Kirche, und die auf dem Kirchhofe Zurückgebliebenen schrieen ihr entgegen, was sie getan hatten, die Hexe
und den Hexenmeister zu fangen und festzuhalten. Ein Schrei
tierischer Wut und Lust erhob sich; einen Kreis schloß das Volk
um die Kirchtüren.

In dem Gotteshause war der Prediger zu dem Meister Konrad
und seiner Tochter getreten; sie vernahmen das Geschrei, und
Ehrn Friedemann bat die Fremden, ein wenig zu harren, bis die
armen, blöden Leute sich nach Haus verlaufen und den Weg
geräumet haben würden. Er ahnete nicht, wie sehr diese Zöge-
rung die dräuende Gefahr verstärkte. Die finstere Vermutung
des lauernden Haufens ward zur Gewißheit; es zweifelte auf
dem Friedhofe nun niemand mehr, daß die Fremden dem Bösen
eigneten, und es war niemand, der nicht mit Eifer einen Brand,
ein Holzscheit oder Reisigbündel zu ihrem Scheiterhaufen getragen hätte.

„Gebannt! gebannt! Sie kann nicht heraus! sie können nicht

staring fixedly at both doors, themselves resembling wicked, malevolent, spiteful spirits and goblins as much as possible. They waited greedily for the end of the service.

Inside the church the preacher, Friedemann Leutenbacher, administered the Body which was broken for the world and the Blood which was shed for it; all the congregation, even those who were to share in the guilt of Else's death, drank from the chalice which the lips of the maiden had touched.

When the minister offered the simple tin vessel to the sweet mouth of the maiden, a feeling of holy ecstasy rippled through him, a sensation of infinite happiness; there was peace in his soul and on the earth; his life had not fallen in the time of the most fearful of all wars. The bliss of an entire existence was consummated in one moment; and when this moment had flown, Friedemann Leutenbacher had no more to expect on this earth.

His congregation rushed out of the church with a rumbling and confused noise, and those who had remained in the churchyard cried out to tell the others what they had done to catch and hold fast the witch and sorcerer. There arose a cry of beastly rage and desire; the people formed a circle around the church doors.

Within the church the preacher had stepped over to Master Conrad and his daughter just as they heard the outcry. The Reverend Friedemann bade the strangers wait a moment until the poor, stupid people had scattered to their homes and cleared the way. He did not suspect how much this delay increased the threatening danger; the evil presumption of the lurking mob became a reality. No one in the churchyard doubted any longer that the strangers were in league with the devil, and there was no one who would not have zealously carried a firebrand, a piece of wood, or a fagot to their pyre.

"Bewitched! Bewitched! She can't get out!

heraus! Hex! Hex! Hex! In Christi Namen wollen wir sie nicht mehr dulden! Gebannt! gebannt!" lief's von Mund zu Mund, und immer wilder wurden Mienen und Gebärden. Man riß Stöcke aus den Hecken und Zäunen, man griff Steine vom Boden auf; aus den nächsten Hütten holte man Äxte, Dreschflegel und Mistgabeln.—

„Gebannt, gebannt! Hex, Hex, Hex! Sie können nicht heraus, holt sie, schlagt sie, ins Feuer mit der Zauberschen und dem Hexenmeister!"—

„Sie weichen nicht; lasset uns gehen; sie werden nicht wagen, uns anzufallen", sagte der Meister Konrad, und Else nickte und flüsterte: „Gott wird uns schützen, jetzt wie immer; ja, lasset uns gehen!"

Den Pfarrer faßte eine fürchterliche Angst; schon hatten sich der Vater und die Tochter gegen die Pforte gewendet, und er konnte nur so schnell als möglich an ihre Seite eilen, ihnen durch seine Gegenwart und Autorität Schutz zu geben.

Zwischen dem Vater und dem Prediger trat Else von der Tanne auf die Schwelle; aber all ihr Mut sank vor dem Geschrei, dem Geheul, mit welchem sie empfangen wurde. Das Blut wich aus ihren Wangen und flutete ängstlich in wilder Hast nach dem Herzen zurück. Sie wankte und faßte krampfhaft den Arm ihres Vaters, und durch die nahenden Ohnmachtsschauer vernahm sie dumpf das widrig-abscheuliche Geheul und den schrecklichen Ruf:

„Hex! Hex! Hex! Schlage tot! schlage tot!"

Mit erhobenen Händen sprang der Prediger Friedemann Leutenbacher in seinem schwarzen Chorrock vor und rief um Frieden und schrie, daß er sprechen wolle, daß man ihn hören solle.

Seine Gemeinde jedoch, gepackt und geschüttelt vom Wahnsinn der Zeit,—seine Gemeinde, außer sich, toll, rasend, wußte nichts mehr von irgendeinem Band, das sie an Himmel und Erde fesselte. Der Ruf des Pfarrers verhallte ohnmächtig, wirkungslos in dem Tumult, dem Geschrei nach dem Blute der beiden Fremden.

Witch! Witch! Witch! In the name of Christ we will not tolerate them any longer! Bewitched! Bewitched!" ran from mouth to mouth, and wilder and wilder became their mien and behavior. They broke sticks from the hedges and fences, they picked up stones from the ground; they fetched axes, flails, and pitchforks from the neighboring huts.

"Bewitched! Bewitched! Witch! Witch! Witch! They can't get out! Seize them! Hit them! Into the fire with the little sorceress and the magician."

"They are not leaving; let us go. They will not dare to attack us," said Master Conrad, and Else nodded and whispered,

"God will protect us now as always; yes, let us go."

A fearful anxiety seized the minister. The father and daughter had already turned toward the exit, and he could only hurry to their side as quickly as possible in order to give them protection through his presence and authority.

Else von der Tanne stepped upon the threshold between her father and the preacher; but all her courage sank before the outcry and the screams with which they were received. The blood left her cheeks and flooded anxiously in wild haste back to her heart. She wept and grasped the arm of her father convulsively, and through the increasing feeling of faintness, she dully perceived the repulsive howling and the terrible cry:

"Witch! Witch! Witch! Kill her! Kill her!"

The preacher, Friedemann Leutenbacher, sprang forward in his black surplice with raised hands, and called for peace; he cried out that he wished to speak and to be heard.

But his congregation, seized and agitated by the frenzy of the time—his congregation, beside themselves, frantic, raving—were no longer conscious of any tie that bound them to heaven and earth. The cry of the minister died away faintly without effect amid the tumult, amid the outcry for the blood of the two strangers.

„Schlage tot! Schlage tot! Reißt sie von der Schwelle, reißt sie vom Gottesacker—stürzt sie in den Mühlenteich! Schlage tot! Hex, Hex! Schlage tot!"

Stöcke und Steine, Erdklöße von den Gräbern, Totengebeine, welche die Schaufel des Totengräbers aufgeworfen hatte, alles, was zur Hand war, wurde gegen den Meister Konradus, sein Kind und den Pfarrherrn von Wallrode im Elend geschleudert. Und aus der Hand des Buben, welcher den dürren Zweig vom Galgenbaume brach, die Hexe und Unholdin in die Kirche zu bannen, flog ein scharfkantiger Kiesel und traf die Jungfrau auf die linke Brust, daß sie mit einem Schrei zusammenbrach und bewußtlos in die Arme des Vaters sank. Einige Tropfen roten Blutes traten auf ihre Lippen, und gräßlich jauchzte das Volk, als es die schlanke, herrliche Gestalt zusammenknicken und sinken sah. Aber mit einem Schrei, der schier nicht aus einer Menschenbrust zu kommen schien, sah der Pfarrer Friedemann Leutenbacher Else von der Tanne fallen und das Blut über ihre Lippen brechen. Auch er vergaß sich, wie sein Dorf, er kannte sich nicht mehr; tausend Fratzen tanzten vor seinen Augen, alle die Narben, die er an seinem Körper und in seiner Seele trug, brannten in diesem Augenblick wie höllisches Feuer; vom Wahnsinn gepackt und geschüttelt wurde auch er. Von den Stufen der Kirchtür war er herabgesprungen, mit gewaltiger Faust hatte er den Mörder Elses von der Tanne zu Boden geschlagen und verfolgte mit einem Totengräberspaten, den er einer andern Hand entriß, das entsetzte Volk über die Gräber. Verwirrt, betäubt, verstört entfloh die Menge, und der Gottesacker war leer;—nur aus der Ferne blickten die atemlosen Bewohner von Wallrode stier und starr nach der Pforte des Friedhofes und nach der Mauer, die ihn umschloß. Schaudernd erwachend ließ der Prediger den Spaten sinken und knieete mit dem Vater neben der verwundeten Jungfrau.

Bleich und regungslos, mit geschlossenen Augen, doch ohne den geringsten Zug des Schmerzes im Gesicht, lag Else von der Tanne auf den Stufen der Kirchtür in den Armen ihres

"Kill her! Kill her! Tear her from the threshold! Tear her from the graveyard! Throw her into the mill-pond! Kill her! Witch! Witch! Kill her!"

Sticks and stones, clods of earth from the graves, bones of dead men that the shovel of the gravedigger had thrown up; everything that was at hand was hurled at Master Conrad, his child, and the pastor of Wallrode in Elend. And from the hand of the boy that had broken the dry branch from the gallows-tree in order to charm the witch and sorceress in the church, there flew a sharp-edged piece of stone, which struck the maiden upon the left breast so that she collapsed with an outcry, and sank unconscious into the arms of her father. Some drops of red blood appeared on her lips and the people exulted horridly, when they saw the slender, splendid figure collapse and sink down. But with a cry that did not seem at all to come from a human breast, the minister, Friedemann Leutenbacher, watched Else von der Tanne fall and the blood break over her lips. He too, like his village, forgot himself, no longer knew himself. A thousand caricatures danced before his eyes; all the scars he bore on his body and in his soul burned in this moment like hellish fire. He too was seized and agitated by frenzy. He sprang from the steps of the church door, and with a powerful fist struck down the murderer of Else von der Tanne, and with a gravedigger's spade, which he tore from the hand of another, he pursued the terrified folk across the graves. Confused, stunned, bewildered, the crowd fled, and the God's-acre was left empty. Only from a distance did the breathless inhabitants of Wallrode watch, fixed and staring, the gate of the cemetery and the wall which enclosed it. Awakening with a shudder the preacher dropped the spade and knelt with the father beside the wounded maiden.

Pale and motionless, Else von der Tanne lay on the steps of the church door in the arms of her father, her eyes closed, yet without the slightest expression of pain upon her face.

Vaters. Die kleinen Vögel, welche der Lärm aus den Bäumen des Friedhofs verscheucht hatte, kamen zurück, hüpften von Zweig zu Zweig und reckten zwitschernd die Hälse und sahen neugierig herab auf die stille, traurige Gruppe, wußten sie aber sowenig zu deuten wie den Aufruhr und das schreckhafte Getös vorhin: harmlos spielten sie ihr heiteres Sommerdasein im Sonnenlicht und grünen Gezweig weiter. Der Magister und der Prediger trugen die bewußtlose Jungfrau zuerst in das Pfarrhaus, wo sie den heißen Tag über lag und niemand kannte. Erst als der Abend nahete, erwachte sie und seufzte tief und sah fragend sich um. Langsam kam die Erinnerung, und als sie kam, schloß Else schaudernd und erzitternd die holden Augen zum zweitenmal. In der sanften Kühle des Abends trugen der Meister Konrad und der Pfarrer Friedemann Leutenbacher die verwundete Maid auf ihren Wunsch in den Wald zurück, und alles Jammers waren sie voll.

Niemand folgte ihnen als das alte Weiblein, welches schon am frühen Morgen am Wege saß und so warnend sang. So rot war der Schein der Abendsonne, daß man nicht sah, wie bleich, wie bleich die Stirn der Jungfrau war;—als die Träger der leichten Last die ersten Bäume des großen Waldes erreichten, ging der Mond auf, und das Reh stand und wartete auf die Herrin.———

„Er hat mich in Finsternis gelegt, wie die Toten in der Welt!" wiederholte Ehrn Friedemann Leutenbacher zu Wallrode im Elend, trat an seinen Tisch und zeichnete drei Kreuze unter die Predigt für das Weihnachtsfest des Jahres sechzehnhundertachtundvierzig. Martina hatte jetzt das Lämpchen auf den Tisch gestellt, ohne deshalb anzufragen, sie hatte auch einen Laib Brod und ein Messer neben die Predigt gelegt;—die weiße Katze saß aufrecht im Stuhl des Pfarrers und sah mit grünlich leuchtenden Augen in das Licht und auf das Brod. In diesem Augenblick pochte jemand an das Fenster, und Ehrn Friedemann fuhr zusammen, als habe ihn die Hand des Todes berührt. Einen kurzen Moment zögerte er, dann aber öffnete er das Fenster, welches der Wind ihm fast aus der Hand riß. Heulend drang der

The little birds which had been frightened from the trees by the noise in the graveyard returned, hopping from branch to branch, stretching their necks amid great twittering, and looking curiously down at the quiet, melancholy group; but they could no better understand it than the frightful uproar and the din which had gone before. Innocently they continued to lead their cheerful summer existence in the sunlight and greenery. At first the teacher and the minister carried the unconscious maiden into the parsonage, where she lay during the entire hot day, without recognizing anyone. Only when evening approached did she awaken; she sighed deeply, glancing questioningly about her. Slowly her memory returned, and when it returned, Else shut her fair eyes shudderingly and tremblingly for the second time. According to her wish Master Conrad and the minister, Friedemann Leutenbacher, carried the wounded maiden back into the forest in the soft coolness of the evening, and they were filled with despair.

No one followed them, save the little old woman who had been sitting by the roadside early that morning and who had sung so admonishingly. So red was the light of the evening sun that they did not see how pale, how very pale the forehead of the maiden had become. When the bearers of the light burden reached the first trees of the great forest, the moon was rising, and the roe stood waiting for its mistress.

"He hath set me in dark places, as them that be dead in the world," repeated the Reverend Friedemann Leutenbacher of Wallrode in Elend, stepping to his desk, and drawing three crosses below the sermon for the Christmas festival of the year sixteen hundred and forty-eight. Martina had by now placed the little lamp upon the desk, without asking if she should; she also put down a loaf of bread and a knife beside the sermon. The white cat was sitting upright in the minister's chair and was looking with green, shining eyes at the light and at the bread. At this moment someone rapped at the window, and the Reverend Friedemann started as if the hand of death had touched him. He hesitated a brief moment, but then opened the window, which the wind almost took out of his hand. Howling,

Sturm in das Gemach und trieb den Schnee bis auf den Tisch. Die Lampe erlosch, die Blätter der Predigt wurden durcheinandergeworfen und in die Ecken gewirbelt; mit einem entsetzten Satz verkroch sich die Katze unter dem Ofen.

„Wer ist da? was will man zu solcher Stund?" rief der Pastor; zwei dürre Hände klammerten sich an das Fensterkreuz, und eine alte, keuchende Stimme kreischte:

„Gebet mir ein Stück Brod für meine Nachricht: Else von der Tanne muß sterben in dieser Nacht." Der Pfarrer von Wallrode sprach kein Wort, er fiel schwer nieder auf beide Kniee und faßte ebenfalls das Fensterkreuz mit beiden Händen. Die Stimme draußen fuhr fort:

„Die schöne Else muß sterben, ich aber kann's nicht; gebet mir ein Stücklein Brod. Der Wolf ist mir ausgewichen auf meinem Weg, der fallende Ast hat mich nicht treffen dürfen, der Schnee hat mich nicht verschüttet im wilden Walde. Ich bin so alt, so alt—und die schöne junge Else muß sterben. Gebet mir ein Stück Brod!"

Der Prediger hatte sich wieder erhoben, er tastete mechanisch und reichte dem gespenstischen Wesen da draußen, welches die schöne junge Else um den Tod beneidete, den schwarzen Laib und das Messer.

„Im Namen Gottes und aller seiner guten Geister Dank!" kreischte die Stimme, und dann kam ein neuer Sturmesstoß und jagte solche neue gewaltige Lasten des Schnees heran, daß die Lichter der Hütten dem Pfarrhaus gegenüber gänzlich verschwanden. Nun war es fast, als habe der Sturm das alte Weib wieder entführt, wie er es brachte.

Vergeblich rief der Prediger den Namen desselben, der Schall seiner Stimme ging in dem Brausen und Zischen verloren. Niemand antwortete, eine Minute lang war's dem Pfarrer, als ob es gar keine Menschenstimme, nicht die Stimme jenes alten Weibes, das am Johannistag am Wege saß, gewesen sei, welche ihm das Wort, daß Else von der Tanne sterbe, ins Fenster gekreischt habe. Ein böser Geist, welcher auf den Sturmwolken fuhr, hatte

the storm swept into the chamber, driving the snow up to the table. The lamp went out; the leaves of the sermon were thrown into confusion and whirled into the corners; with a terrified leap the cat ran and hid under the stove.

"Who is there? What do you want at such an hour?" cried the pastor. Two withered hands clutched at the cross-bar of the window, and an old, gasping voice shrilled:

"Give me a piece of bread for my message; Else von der Tanne must die tonight!" The minister of Wallrode spoke not a word, he fell heavily upon both knees, and likewise grasped the cross-bar of the window with both hands. The voice outside continued:

"The beautiful Else must die, but I cannot. Give me a piece of bread. The wolf avoided me on my way; the falling branch was not allowed to strike me; the snow did not bury me in the wild forest. I am so old, so old, and the young and beautiful Else must die. Give me a piece of bread!"

The preacher had arisen again; he groped mechanically, and handed the black loaf and the knife to the ghostly creature out there that coveted the death of the young and beautiful Else.

"In the name of God and all His good spirits, thanks," shrieked the voice, and then there came a new blast of the storm, driving before it such new and mighty burdens of the snow that the lights of the huts opposite the parsonage vanished entirely. Now it almost seemed as if the storm whisked the old woman away again just as it had brought her.

In vain the preacher called her name, but the sound of his voice was lost in the roaring and hissing. No one answered. For the duration of a minute the minister felt as if it had been no human voice at all, not the voice of that old woman who was sitting by the roadway on the day of St. John which had shrieked the news into his window that Else von der Tanne was dying. An evil spirit that was borne on the storm clouds had

es ihm ins Ohr geschrieen; eine Menschenstimme konnte solch
kalt, grimmig Erschrecken nicht einjagen, konnte solche furchtbare Vernichtung nicht bringen.

Else, die schöne, junge Else stirbt! Else stirbt! Else stirbt!—
Der Pfarrer von Wallrode im Elend faßte mit beiden Händen
die Stirn—war es doch Wahrheit? War die Stunde da, die kommen mußte? War die Stunde gekommen, die seit dem Tage Johannis des Täufers langsam, drohend, unabwendbar heran-
schlich?

„Sie stirbt—Else von der Tanne stirbt!" stöhnte der Pfarrherr. Er tastete nach der Tür und wankte hinaus.

Auf dem Flur stand Martina mit ihrer Lampe.

„Um Jesu willen, Ehrwürden, was ist Euch geschehen? was
wollt Ihr tun? Ehrwürden, wollt Ihr fort? Bei diesem Wetter?"

Ehrn Friedemann schien die treue Dienerin gar nicht zu erblicken; er ging an ihr vorüber, er stand vor dem Haus im
Sturm und tiefen Schnee; mit dem Mantel verhüllte er das Gesicht und schritt durch das Dorf, dem Wind und Flockengewir-
bel entgegen, dem Walde zu. Das Gebell der Hofhunde verhallte hinter ihm; er war allein mit seinen wilden Gedanken in
der wilden Nacht.

Von dem freien Felde zwischen dem Dorf und dem Forste
hatte der Wind den Schnee so rein weggefegt, daß der kahle,
schwarze Boden nackt in dem seltsamen Dämmer dalag, und
entsetzlich war dieser Wind auf diesem Gange. Er trieb den
Atem in die Brust zurück, als wolle er sie zersprengen, wütend
griff er in die Haare, die Mantelfalten des Wanderers, um ihn
zu Boden zu werfen, in rasenden Sprüngen und Sätzen schnaubte
er gegen das Dorf Wallrode hinab und jagte das weiße Gestäube vor sich hin.

Als der Pfarrherr den Rand des Waldes erreichte, hätte er
sich selber zu Boden werfen mögen, um die keuchende Brust
ausatmen zu lassen. Wie Schlachtendonner rollte es durch das
Gebirge—Geächz und Stöhnen, Gekrach und Geknirsch, wie
von den Grenzen der Erde her!

190

screamed it into his ear. A human voice could not induce such a cold, bitter fear, or produce such fearful annihilation.

Else, the young and beautiful Else is dying! Else is dying! Else is dying! The minister of Wallrode in Elend clasped his forehead with both his hands:—could it be the truth after all? Could the hour have come which had to come? Had the hour come which had been creeping on slowly, threateningly, inevitably since the day of St. John the Baptist?

"She is dying! Else von der Tanne is dying!" groaned the curate. He groped for the door and stumbled out.

Martina was standing in the hall with her lamp.

"For Heaven's sake, Your Reverence, what has happened to you? What are you going to do? Are you going out, Your Reverence? In such weather?"

The Reverend Friedemann did not seem to see the faithful servant at all. He passed by her, and stood in front of the house in the storm and in the deep snow; covering his face with his cloak, he walked through the village against the wind and swirling flakes toward the forest. The barking of the watch dogs died away behind him; he was alone with his wild thoughts in the wild night.

The wind had swept away the snow so thoroughly from the open field between the village and the forest that the fallow, black earth lay bare in the strange gloom, and terrible was the wind on this path. It drove the breath back into the breast as if to burst it; raging, it grasped the hair and the folds of the minister's cloak to throw him to the earth. In frenzied leaps and bounds it raged blustering at the village of Wallrode, driving before it the white snow-dust.

When the minister reached the edge of the forest he would have gladly thrown himself upon the ground in order to regain his gasping breath. The storm roared through the mountains like the thunder of battle, moaning and groaning, grating and cracking as if coming from the ends of the earth.

Wo das hübsche Reh die blutende Else mit fröhlichen Sprüngen and Schmeichelgebärden empfing, lag der Schnee mannshoch; im Walde konnte der Sturm nicht also sein Spiel mit ihm treiben;— in manchen Gründen war die Luft so still wie hinter einer hohen Mauer, und nur das Gebrüll zu Häupten und das Ächzen und Wiegen der Stämme war hier ein Zeichen, wie's von Wipfel zu Wipfel, von einer Höhe zur andern in die Ebene hinausfuhr.

Die Kinder und die Irren hält Gottes Hand fest auf ihren Wegen—seinen Weg durch den verschneiten Wald konnte der Pfarrer von Wallrode nur durch ein Wunder finden. In seinem zerrütteten Gehirn war jetzt seltsamerweise nur alles liebliche Frühlings- und Sommerglück der letzten elf Jahre lebendig. Wo er brusttief in dem aufgehäuften Schnee versank, da hatte die kleine Else aus den Stengeln der gelben Butterblumen Ketten geschlungen und das uralte Kinderlied vom guten Bischof Buko von Halberstadt den Pastor von Wallrode gelehrt. Wo die große Eiche, die tausend Jahre lang allen Ungewittern trotzte, niedergebrochen war, hatte Else von der Tanne in jungfräulicher Schöne ruhig und still gestanden und dem fernen, fernen Rollen und Donnern in der Ebene gelauscht, wo die Schweden unter ihrem Generalleutnant Königsmark sich mit den Kaiserlichen jagten. Vor dem Eingange der schwarzen Höhle, in welcher sich die Gemeinde, um der Wut des Feindes im Jahre sechzehnhundertneununddreißig zu entgehen, verborgen hatte, stand ein Wolf; aber er griff den irrenden Wanderer sowenig an, wie er die irre Justine angegriffen hatte; mit winselndem Geheul wich er in das Innere der Grube zurück.

Als der Prediger in den Bezirk der hohen Tanne gelangte, hörte das Sausen und Brausen in den Lüften und Wipfeln plötzlich auf, und als Friedemann Leutenbacher das Licht der Hütte des Meisters Konrad durch die Stämme schimmern sah, endete auch der Schneefall, und es wurde nach all dem Aufruhr zwischen Himmel und Erde ganz still. Aber in dieser unerwarteten gespenstischen Pause fühlte der nächtliche Wanderer erst im vollsten Maße die übermenschlichen Anstrengungen und Mühen des

191

Where the beautiful roe had received the bleeding Else with joyous leaps and flattering gestures, the snow was over a man's head; in the forest the storm could thus not carry on its game with him; in many a glen the air was as still as if behind a high wall and only the roaring overhead and the groaning and swaying of the tree-trunks was here an indication of how the wind was blowing among the tree-tops and from one height to another out into the plain.

God's hand guides children and deranged men on their way. Only through a miracle could the minister of Wallrode find his way through the snow-bound forest. Strangely enough the only thing still vivid in his distracted mind was all the pleasant spring and summer happiness of the last eleven years. Where he sank breast deep in the drifted snow, at that very place the little Else had woven chains with the stems of yellow buttercups and had taught the pastor of Wallrode the ancient children's song about the good Bishop Buko of Halberstadt. Where the great oak that had defied all manner of storms for a thousand years had crashed down, there Else von der Tanne had stood quietly and silently in virginal beauty, listening to the far away rolling and thundering on the plain where the Swedes under their lieutenant-general, Koenigsmark, were clashing with the Imperials. A wolf stood before the entrance of the black cave in which his parishioners had hidden to escape the rage of the enemy in the year sixteen hundred and thirty; but it no more attacked the straying wanderer than it had attacked the deranged Justine. With a whining howl it drew back into the interior of the cave.

When the preacher reached the vicinity of the tall fir tree, the blustering and roaring in the tree-tops and open spaces suddenly ceased, and when Friedemann Leutenbacher saw the light of Master Conrad's hut glimmering between the tree-trunks, the falling of the snow also ceased, and after all the uproar between heaven and earth, it became quite still. But during this unexpected, ghost-like pause the nightly wanderer felt for the first time in the fullest measure the superhuman exertions and efforts

zurückgelegten Pfades. Die Pulse klopften, die Kniee und Hände erzitterten, mit einem tiefen Seufzer griff Friedemann Leutenbacher nach einem überhängenden Baumzweig, um sich aufrechtzuerhalten. Heiß und keuchend war sein Atem, seine Augen, von der Gewalt des Windes ausgetrocknet, brannten, rings um ihn her belebte sich die Schneedämmerung und die Finsternis des Forstes mit tausendfachen wirbelnden Gestalten seiner fiebernden Phantasie—er hätte in seiner Angst laut aufschreien mögen und vermochte doch keinen Laut hervorzubringen! Es war ihm, als kämpfe er noch immer gegen den Sturm und die Gefahren des Weges an, um das ruhige Licht in der Hütte zu erreichen; und es war ihm, als weiche dieses Licht immer weiter, weiter, weiter zurück; und es war ihm, als werde er ihm in alle Ewigkeit so zum Tode erschöpft und in solch namenloser Angst folgen müssen.

Dieser Zustand währte wohl eine Viertelstunde lang; dann endete er, wie der Sturm geendet hatte.

„Else von der Tanne stirbt! Else von der Tanne ist tot!" sagte der Prediger von Wallrode im Elend mit tonloser Stimme und schritt durch den Raum, der ihn von der Hütte des Meisters Konrad trennte.

Nur fußtief lag der Schnee hier zwischen den Stämmen, aber gegen die Hütte selbst war er in desto gewaltigeren Massen getrieben worden. Der Pfarrherr von Wallrode vermochte es kaum, sich einen Weg zu dem niedern, engen Fenster zu bahnen; endlich gelang es ihm doch, und er stand und blickte stier und starr in das Gemach, allein die Scheiben waren so sehr vom Frosthauch beschlagen, daß er nur unbestimmte Schatten sah; er mußte die mühevolle Arbeit von neuem beginnen, um zu der Tür der Hütte zu gelangen.

Er pochte, doch zuerst regte sich nichts darinnen; er pochte zum zweiten Male, und dann hörte er den schweren Tritt des Magisters.

„Wer ist da? Hierinnen ist der Tod—das Leben ist entwichen aus diesem Haus."

192

of the path he had come. His pulse throbbed; his hands and knees trembled. With a deep sigh Friedemann Leutenbacher clutched at an overhanging branch of a tree to hold himself erect. His breath was hot and gasping; his eyes, dried by the force of the wind, were burning; all around him the snowy twilight and the gloom of the forest came alive with a thousand whirling figures of his feverish imagination. He would fain have cried aloud in his anxiety, and yet was unable to utter any sound. It seemed to him as if he were still fighting against the storm and the perils of the way in order to reach the peaceful light in the hut; and it seemed to him as if that light kept receding farther and farther; and it seemed to him as if he would have to follow it into all eternity, exhausted unto death and seized with nameless anxiety.

This condition lasted perhaps a quarter hour; then it ended just as the storm had ended.

"Else von der Tanne is dying! Else von der Tanne is dead!" said the preacher of Wallrode in Elend as he walked through the space which separated him from the hut of Master Conrad.

The snow lay only ankle-deep here between the tree-trunks, but had been driven in great masses against the hut itself. The pastor of Wallrode was hardly able to clear a path for himself to the low narrow window. But he finally succeeded, and stood looking fixed and staring into the room; but the panes were so encrusted with frost that he was only able to see indefinite silhouettes; he had to begin the exhausting work anew in order to reach the door of the hut.

He knocked, but at first there was no movement inside; he knocked a second time, and then he heard the heavy footstep of the scholar.

"Who is there? Inside here is Death. Life has departed from this house."

„Öffne, Vater", sagte der Prediger von Wallrode.

Der Meister Konradus schob den Riegel zurück, und Friede-
mann Leutenbacher trat in die Hütte; stumm wandte sich der
Meister, und Friedemann stand vor der Leiche Elses von der
Tanne.

— — — — — — — — — — — — — — — — — — — — — — —

Sie lag auf ihrem Lager wie eine Schlafende; der Vater hatte
ihr bereits die Arme über der Brust ins Kreuz gelegt; sie schien
zu lächeln, und die Ruhe des bleichen Gesichtes war mehr als
jegliches Mienenspiel irdischen Behagens, irdischen Glückes.

Das zahme Reh stand neben dem Bett und hatte seinen schlan-
ken Hals, sein Köpfchen auf die Decke gelegt, die weiße Wald-
taube, welche vor zwei Jahren aus dem Neste gefallen und von
Else aufgezogen war, saß zu Häupten des Lagers auf dem Bett-
pfosten und sah auf die bleiche Herrin.

„Um fünf Uhr, als der Sturm anhub, ist sie gestorben", sagte
der Vater. „Ich dachte nicht, daß es so bald sein würde; sie ist
aber ohne Schmerzen fortgegangen, hat den großen Sturm nicht
mehr erlebt;——sie ist tot."

„Sie ist tot!" wiederholte Friedemann Leutenbacher, der
Pfarrherr zu Wallrode im Elend, und kniete neben dem Lager
nieder. Der Meister Konrad setzte die Lampe, welche er bis
jetzt über das stille Haupte der Tochter hielt, auf den Schemel
und stand in der Dämmerung am Fußende des Bettes, ohne sich
zu regen.

Ohne das Gesicht zu erheben, sprach der Prediger nach einer
Weile:

„Saget mir mehr von ihrem Abscheiden, Vater; als ich gestern
abend Abschied nahm, sagte sie, sie würde leben, eine Stimme
in ihrem Herzen habe es ihr versprochen."

Der Vater neigte das Haupt:

„Sie lebt—die Stimme, welche sie vernahm, spricht keine
Lügen. Sie lebt; wir aber sind tot und werden sie nimmer wie-
dersehen."

"Open, father," said the preacher of Wallrode.

Master Conrad pushed back the bolt, and Friedemann Leutenbacher stepped into the hut. The scholar turned around without a word, and Friedemann stood before the corpse of Else von der Tanne.

———  ——  ——  ——  ——  ——  ——  ——  ——  ——  ——  ——  ——  ——  ——  —— ——

She was lying on her couch like one asleep; the father had already crossed her arms over her breast. She seemed to smile, and the peaceful look of her pallid face was more than any expression of earthly comfort or earthly happiness.

The tame roe was standing near the bed and had laid its slender neck and small head upon the covers. The white ringdove, which had fallen out of its nest two years ago and had been reared by Else, sat at the head of the couch on the bedpost, regarding its pallid mistress.

"At five o'clock, when the storm began, she died," said the father. "I did not think that it would be so soon; but she departed without any pain and she did not live to see the great storm—— she is dead."

"She is dead!" repeated Friedemann Leutenbacher, the curate of Wallrode in Elend, kneeling down beside the couch. Master Conrad set the lamp, which he had been holding until now over the motionless head of his daughter, on the footstool and stood in the dusk at the foot of the bed without moving.

Without raising his face, the preacher said after awhile,

"Tell me more of her departing, father; when I left her yesterday, she said that she would live—that a voice in her heart had promised her."

The father bowed his head:

"She lives. The voice that she heard does not lie. She lives; but we are dead and shall never see her again."

Ein Schauer lief über den Leib des Predigers; der Meister
Konrad fuhr fort:

„In der vergangenen Nacht litt sie große Schmerzen; ich hielt
ihre Hand und wich nicht von ihr, bis zum Morgen. Als der
Morgen kam, schlief sie ein und schlummerte wohl drei Stun-
den; dann erwachte sie, grüßte mich und wußte nichts mehr von
den Qualen der Nacht. Sie sorgte um ihre Tiere, Reh und Täub-
lein, und sah sie neben ihrem Bett essen. Ich aber sah, daß sie
kränker war denn je; sie selber wollte weder essen noch trinken,
ihre Stimme war wie ein Hauch. Sie sprach von dem heiligen
Feste und sorgte um Euere Predigt, so Ihr, Friedemann, dem
armen Volke im Dorfe zur Weihnacht halten würdet. Er soll
meiner nicht gedenken, sprach sie,—die Liebe Gottes ist über
allem;—er soll das Vergangene von sich werfen und soll der
Kinder gedenken und zu den Alten reden wie zu den Kindern.
Wir sind so glücklich, glücklich gewesen in ihrem Walde, und als
sie die Steine auf uns warfen und mich trafen, wußten sie nicht,
was sie taten. Er soll um meinetwillen den armen Leuten nicht
länger zürnen, redete sie weiter, ich werde es gewißlich in meinem Herzen fühlen, wenn er morgen hart zu ihnen spricht.——
Ich erinnerte sie an das Versprechen, so Ihr über dieses ihr
gestern gegeben hattet, und sie lächelte und sagte, sie wisse es.
Um Mittag kam die alte Justine, die seit dem Johannistage ihre
Freundin ist, um sich an unserm Herde zu wärmen, und die
blieb bei uns bis zu einbrechender Dämmerung. Da der Kran-
ken Zustand nicht schlechter geworden zu sein schien, so war
allmählich wieder Ruhe in meine Seele gekommen, und ich saß
am Fenster und hatte Platonis hohes Buch Phädon vor mir auf-
geschlagen; die Sanduhr zeigte vier Uhr nach Mittage an. Da
tat die Justine plötzlich einen Schrei und hob beide Arme, und
ich war aufgesprungen und sah auf meine Tochter.

‚Der Tod! der grimme Tod!‘ schrie die Alte im Wahnsinn
und stürzte aus der Hütt hinaus in den Wald und floh wie gejagt von tausend Larven und Schrecknissen; aber meinem Kind
saß der Tod am Herzen. Heimtückisch war er herangeschlichen,

194

A tremor ran through the body of the preacher. Master Conrad continued:

"Last night she was in great pain. I held her hand and did not leave her until morning. When morning came, she fell asleep and slept about three hours; then she awakened, greeted me, and did not remember the agonies of the night. She was anxious about her animals, the roe and the dove, and watched them eat beside her bed. But I saw that she was more ill than ever; she herself would neither eat nor drink, and her voice was like a breath. She spoke of the holy festival, and was concerned about the sermon which you, Friedemann, would preach to the poor people of the village for Christmas. 'He should not think of me,' she said, 'the love of God is over all. He should cast off the past from himself and think of the children, and speak to the old people as if to children. We are so happy, have been so very happy in their forest, and when they threw the stones at us, and hit me, they did not know what they were doing. He should no longer be angry with the poor people on my account,' she spoke further, 'I shall certainly feel it in my heart if he speaks harshly to them tomorrow.' —I reminded her of the promise that you had given her yesterday concerning this, and she smiled, saying she knew it. At noon old Justine, who had been her friend since the day of St. John, came to warm herself at our hearth, and she remained with us until the falling of twilight. Since the condition of the sick maiden did not seem to have grown worse, peace had gradually returned to my mind, and I sat by the window with Plato's great book *Phaedo* open in front of me. The hour-glass indicated four o'clock in the afternoon. Then Justine suddenly uttered a cry, and raised both arms, and I jumped up and looked at my daughter.

" 'Death! Grim Death!' cried the old woman in a frenzy, and rushed out of the hut into the forest as if chased by a thousand spectres and terrors. But Death sat upon the heart of my child. It had crept up stealthily,

und ich hatte es nicht gemerkt. Sie lag mit offenen Augen und sah mich an, wie sie es noch nie getan hatte;—sie regte sich nicht, sie sprach nicht mehr; aber sie kannte mich und wollte mich durch ihre Augen trösten;—gegen fünf Uhr ist sie gestorben. Ich habe sie vergeblich in der Wildnis verborgen—weh, es ist keine Rettung in der Welt vor der Welt——um fünf Uhr ist sie gestorben, und der große Sturm erhob seine Stimme im Wald, sie aber hörte dieselbe nicht;—sie ist sicher und lebt; aber wehe uns!"

Jetzt erhob der Prediger von Wallrode im Elend das Gesicht von der Leiche; er ließ die Hand auf den kalten Händen der toten Else liegen und rief:

„Jawohl, wehe uns! Es ist geschehen—Gottes Wille ist vollbracht. Er hat seine Hand abgezogen von der Erde, er hat die Völker verstoßen und uns vernichtet; es ist keine Hoffnung und kein Licht mehr in der Welt und wird auch nimmer wiederkommen. Wir haben uns gesträubet gegen seine mächtige Hand und sind geschlichen wie Diebe in der Nacht mit unserm und der Erde letztem Schatz und Edelstein, ihn seinem Auge zu verbergen: Er aber hat uns aufgefunden, über uns gehauchet und uns geschlagen mit der Geißel des Zornes; er hat unser gelachet und gegriffen, was sein war. Wer will sich nun fürder wehren? Es ist nicht nütze und verlohnet der Mühe nicht! Lasset der Sünde und der Schande Strom schießen und brausen!—Wer will noch Dämme bauen gegen des Herrn Willen? Der Herr spottet der Erde, und seinem Lachen lauschet der Antichrist in der Tiefe, stehet und ruft den Seinen: Wacht auf, wachet auf, ihr Fürsten der Nacht!—Der Schein Gottes gehet aus der Welt; stehet zu den Riegeln, ihr Gewaltigen, die Pforten des Abgrundes aufzuwerfen,—unser ist das Reich!"

„Der Schein Gottes ist für uns aus der Welt gegangen—für uns ist das letzte Fünklein erloschen. Mein Kind lebt; aber wir, die wir Atem holen, liegen unter dem Fuße des Todes."

Friedemann Leutenbacher hatte sich von den Knieen erhoben; noch einmal sah er die tote Else mit einem langen Blick an;

195

and I had not noticed it. She lay with her eyes open and looked at me as she had never done before. She did not move; she spoke no more, but she recognized me and tried to comfort me with her eyes. About five o'clock she died. I have hidden her in vain in the wilderness. Alas! there is no salvation in the world from the world;—at five o'clock she died, and the great storm raised its voice in the forest, but she did not hear it. She is safe, and lives, but woe to us!"

Then the preacher of Wallrode in Elend raised his countenance from the corpse; he let his hands rest upon the cold hands of the dead Else and cried:

"Indeed, woe to us! It has happened. God's will is done. He has withdrawn His hand from the earth. He has cast off the nations and annihilated us; there is no longer any hope or light in the world, and none will ever come again. We have striven against His mighty hand, and have stolen like thieves in the night with the last treasure and jewel of ours and of the earth to hide it from His eyes. But He has sought us out, breathed over us, and struck us with the scourge of His wrath, and laughed at us, and seized what was His. Who would protect himself further now? It is of no avail and is not worth the trouble. Let the flood of sin and shame shoot forth and roar. Who would still build bulwarks against the will of the Lord? The Lord mocks the earth. And the Antichrist hears His laughter in the depths, stands, and calls to his followers:

"Awake, awake, ye princes of the darkness. The glory of God vanishes from the world. Stand at the bolts, O ye Powerful Ones, to throw open the portals of the abyss! The kingdom is ours!

"For us the glory of God has vanished from the world—for us the last little spark is extinguished. My child lives; but we who still breathe are lying under the heel of Death."

Friedemann Leutenbacher had arisen from his knees; once again he cast a lingering glance at the dead Else;

dann schritt er aus der Hütte, und der Magister Konrad machte
keinen Versuch, ihn aufzuhalten; er fragte ihn nicht, wohin er
gehe, er wußte es nicht, daß der Prediger von Wallrode ihn
neben der Leiche der Tochter allein ließ.—

Der Wind hatte seine Stimme wiederum erhoben; doch nicht
so laut denn zuvor. Im Kreise schritt Friedemann Leutenbacher
um die Hütte an der hohen Tanne, rang die Hände und rief den
Namen:

„Else! Else!"

Ihm antwortete niemand, sogar den Widerhall schien der
Schnee im Walde erstickt zu haben. Die Nacht war jetzt so dunkel wie jene andere furchtbare Nacht, deren Nahen der Prediger so wild in seinem Schmerz verkündet hatte. Das Licht in der
Hütte war plötzlich verschwunden, sei's, daß die Lampe erlosch oder daß der Meister Konrad sie an eine andere, verbor-
genere Stelle gesetzt hatte;—Ehrn Friedemann Leutenbacher
verlor sich in der Wildnis.

Er wanderte und wußte nicht wohin.

Durch tiefen Schnee und über kahle Flächen, bergauf und -ab,
weiter und immer weiter jagte ihn die unendliche Angst seiner
Seele. Er fiel und richtete sich empor; er zerriß die Hände und
die Gewänder und das Gesicht an den Dornen; er sank von
neuem zu Boden und sagte abermals:

„Er hat mich in Finsternis geleget, wie die Toten in der Welt."

Allmählich war es bitter kalt geworden, und nur noch einmal
gelang es dem Unglücklichen, sich zu erheben und weiterzu-
schwanken. Ohne es zu wissen, stieg er immer mehr aus den
Tälern empor, zu jener Höhe, von welcher man die weiteste
Aussicht aus dem Walde in das Land hatte, von welcher er Elsen
von der Tanne Städte und Dörfer, Fluß und Bach bis in die weiteste Ferne gedeutet hatte. Er hörte eine ferne Glocke, nannte
den Namen eines Fleckens und strich mit der Hand über die
Stirne und sagte, daß es Mitternacht sei.

Er stand schaudernd in dem pfeifenden eisigen Winde und
legte lauschend die Hand an das Ohr, wie jemand, der erwar-

then he walked out of the hut. And Master Conrad made no attempt to detain him. He did not ask him whither he was going; he was not aware that the preacher of Wallrode was leaving him alone beside the corpse of his daughter.

The wind had raised its voice again, yet not so loud as before. Friedemann Leutenbacher paced in a circle around the hut under the tall fir tree, wringing his hands and calling the name, "Else, Else!"

No one answered him; even the echo seemed to have been stifled in the forest by the snow. The night was now as dark as that other fearful night whose imminence the preacher had so wildly proclaimed in his torment. Whether the lamp was extinguished or whether Master Conrad had set it in another, a more hidden place, the light in the hut had suddenly gone out. And the Reverend Friedemann Leutenbacher was lost in the wilderness.

He was wandering without knowing whither.

Through deep snow and over bare surfaces, up and down hill, farther and farther he was driven by the infinite anxiety of his soul. He fell and rose up; he tore his hands, his garments, and his face on the thorns; he sank once more to the ground and said again,

"He hath set me in dark places, amid them that be dead in the world."

Gradually it had become bitter cold, and only once more was the unfortunate man able to raise himself and stagger farther. Now unwittingly, he climbed up higher and higher out of the valleys to the height from which the farthest view from the forest across the country was to be had, and from which he had pointed out cities and villages, rivers and brooks in the remotest distances to Else von der Tanne. He heard a distant bell and called the name of a hamlet, stroking his forehead with his hand, and saying that it was midnight.

He stood shuddering in the whistling icy wind and, listening intently, he put his hand to his ear like one who

tet, daß man seinen Namen rufen werde. Nachdem er lange
Zeit so gestanden hatte, schüttelte er das Haupt und sank in
sich zusammen.

Sein Kopf ruhte auf einem Felsstück, sein Leib streckte sich
lang, seine Hände mit den blutroten Narben um die Gelenke
kreuzten sich über der Brust—Friedemann Leutenbacher, der
Prediger am Worte Gottes zu Wallrode im Elend, glaubte jetzt,
er liege in seinem Sarge und der Deckel über ihm; während er
aber dumpf darum grübelte, wie es komme, daß er noch von
sich wisse und denke, entschlief er und ging in einem Traume
fort, ging hinüber auf dem Wege, den Else von der Tanne gegangen war.

Seine Wunden waren geheilt, seine Ketten abgefallen, die
Mauern seines Gefängnisses waren gebrochen, und die Pforte
war aufgerissen. Else von der Tanne hatte dem Prediger Friedemann Leutenbacher das Glück gebracht, als ihr Vater sie, ein
hold klein Kindlein, auf dem Arm in den Wald trug, um sie
vor der bösen Welt zu retten; Else von der Tanne hatte das
Glück Friedemann Leutenbachers nicht mit sich fortgenommen,
als der Welt Elend und Jammer sie doch ausfand und ihr das Herz
zerbrach;—Else von der Tanne führte die Seele des Predigers
aus dem Elend mit sich fort in die ewige Ruhe. Ihnen beiden
war das Beste gegeben, was Gott zu geben hatte in dieser
Christnacht des Jahres eintausendsechshundertvierzigundacht.

Der Magister Konradus hat sein Kind begraben mitten in
der Wildnis, fern von den Menschen; des Predigers Leiche aber
haben die Bauern am zweiten Weihnachtstage nach langem
Suchen gefunden, sie aus dem wüsten Walde hinab ins Dorf getragen und sie neben der Kirche in die Erde gelegt.

Der Meister Konrad hat den Winter durch noch in der Hütte
gewohnt um des armen Rehes und der Taube willen; aber im
Frühling, als die Tiere seiner nicht mehr bedurften und endlich
jedermann wußte, daß der Friede geschlossen sei zu Osnabrück,
ist er fortgegangen. Die alte, arme, irre Justine ist ihm am Bet-
telbrunnen begegnet, hat seinen Schatten vor ihm am Boden

was expecting his name to be called. After he had stood thus for a long time, he shook his head and collapsed.

His head rested upon a piece of rock, his body stretched at full length; the hands which bore the blood-red scars on the wrists he crossed on his breast. Friedemann Leutenbacher, the preacher of the Word of God at Wallrode in Elend, believed he was now lying in his own coffin with the cover over him. But while he was brooding how it happened that he was still conscious of himself and could think, he fell asleep and went forth in a dream, went out upon the way which Else von der Tanne had gone.

His wounds were healed, his chains fallen away, the walls of his prison were broken, and the door had been thrown open. Else von der Tanne had brought happiness to the preacher, Friedemann Leutenbacher, when her father bore her, a gracious little child, on his arm into the forest in order to save her from the evil world. Else von der Tanne had not taken the happiness of Friedemann Leutenbacher away with her, when the misery and wretchedness of the world finally sought her out, and broke her heart. Else von der Tanne led the soul of the preacher out of misery away with her into eternal peace. To them both was given the best that God had to give on this Christmas Eve of the year one thousand six hundred and forty-eight.

Master Conrad buried his child in the midst of the wilderness far from men. But the peasants found the corpse of the preacher on the day following Christmas after a long search; they carried it out of the desolate forest into the village, and laid it to rest in the earth beside the church.

Master Conrad lived on in the hut through the winter for the sake of the poor roe and the dove; but in the spring when the animals no longer had need of him, and when finally it was generally known that peace had been concluded at Osnabrueck, he went away. Poor, deranged old Justine met him at the Beggar's Well; she saw his shadow before him on the ground,

und einen schwarzen aufrechten Schatten ihm folgen sehen und gesagt, das letzte sei der Tod gewesen.

Heute sind von dem Dorf Wallrode im Elend nur noch geringe Trümmer im Wald zu erblicken; es ist nicht auszusagen, nicht an den Fingern herzuzählen, was niederging durch diesen deutschen Krieg, welcher dreißig Jahre gedauert hat.

and a black upright shadow following him, and said that the latter was Death.

Today only slight ruins of the village of Wallrode in Elend are still to be seen in the forest. It cannot be fully told or counted on the fingers what was destroyed in this German war that lasted thirty years.

# TRANSLATOR'S NOTES

# TRANSLATOR'S NOTES

(Page references are to the reproduced German text from *Wilhelm Raabe, Sämtliche Werke,* IX, part 1. Numerals before each quoted expression refer to lines of the text. References to Hans Oppermann's "Anmerkungen" are made by citing the author's last name only, followed by the page number.)

*Page 161*

1. *schneiete.* Raabe frequently retains the archaic *e* in conjugated verb forms. N. C. A. Perquin considers the symbolism of snow significant in *Else von der Tanne* (cf. pp. 178, 190, 192 below) as well as in other works of Raabe's. Under the rubric of "die Einheit der Menschheit" he writes: "Wohl manchem wird die Bedeutung des *Schnees* in Raabes Gefühlsleben aufgefallen sein. Einerseits—schon von der *Chronik* an—ist er ihm Freude und ein heiteres Spiel, andererseits aber ist er ein Symbol der Reinheit, der reinen Decke für ein liebes Grab." Perquin finds the same symbolism in *Der Hungerpastor, Holunderblüte, Abu Telfan,* and *Der Schüdderump.* See *Wilhelm Raabes Motive als Ausdruck seiner Weltanschauung* (Amsterdam: H. J. Paris, 1927), p. 222.

5. *Harzwald.* The word *Wald* often means a forested, mountain area in Germany; e.g., *Schwarzwald, Odenwald,* etc. The Harz is such a forested upland, the northernmost in Germany, located between the Weser and the Elbe. Winds sweeping without hindrance across the north German plain cause the climate to be raw and damp the year round. The Harz is well-watered with numerous streams; and in the Upper Harz, the presumed location of the present story, there are numerous ponds. The highest peak is the Brocken (3,806 ft.), famous in legend and as the site of the "Walpurgis Night" scene in Goethe's *Faust.* "The Harz was the last stronghold of paganism in Germany, and to that fact are due its legends and fanciful names." *Encyclopaedia Britannica,* XI, 1969, p. 148. The area is not thickly settled even today.

10. *Decembris.* Latin genitive. Raabe's use of the language here and subsequently adds a note of solemnity to the narrative.

12. *Dominus Magister.* Latin title for clergyman. The second part is a shortened form of *Magister Artium,* Master of Arts. The first is the equivalent of the German *Herr.*

13. *Wallrode in Elend.* Wallrode is an imaginary village. There is, however, an Allrode in the upper Harz, located in a district once called Elend. Today there is a village by the name of Elend near

117

the Brocken. Although Raabe links the name of the district with the meaning of the modern German word which signifies "misery" (see 162:30–31) it is actually derived from the Old High German word *elilenti*, meaning "in a foreign country" or "exiled." (See Friedrich Kluge, *Etymologisches Wörterbuch der deutschen Sprache*, 17th ed., Berlin, 1957, s.v.) Both Goethe and Uhland use *Elend* occasionally in its original sense as an archaism. (See Friedrich Kainz, "Klassik und Romantik," *Deutsche Wortgeschichte*, eds. F. Mauer and F. Stroh, II, Berlin, 1959, pp. 249, 383.) Further, Schiller uses the adjectival form *elend* with the meaning "homeless" or "exiled." (Ibid., p. 255) Cf. the modern German idiom *ins Elend schicken*, meaning "to exile."

15. *darob*. An archaic form for *darüber*.

23. *Imperium Romanum*. The Roman Empire proper. The date 476 A.D. is usually taken as marking the end of the Empire in the West, for in that year Romulus Augustulus, last of the Western emperors, was deposed by the barbarian followers of Odoacer, who was thereupon proclaimed ruler of Italy. This development was, however, merely the culmination of a series of misfortunes inflicted on Rome by the Germanic invaders, the principal one of which was the sack of Rome by Alaric, the Visigoth, in 410 A.D. Raabe's expression "wandernde Völker" is a reference to the great historical movement of the Germanic tribes known as the *Völkerwanderung*.

24–25. *das Römische Reich Deutscher Nation*. The Holy Roman Empire of the German Nation. Raabe has omitted the usual adjective *Heilige* in the title. This is the empire which lasted for more than a thousand years, even if its last stages were ignominious. It had its beginnings with the crowning of Charlemagne by Pope Leo III in Rome on Christmas day 800 A.D. It ended in 1806, when Francis II of Austria gave up the imperial crown. Its specifically German phase commenced, however, in 962 A.D. with the crowning of the German king, Otto I, as emperor in Rome. Charlemagne had not referred to his empire as "Roman," but simply as "Imperium Christianum." Not until Otto II (973–83) was the expression "Romanorum" added to the royal title. The full title developed only in the late Middle Ages.

29–30. *Frieden zu Münster und Osnabrück*. After four years of negotiations, peace treaties ending the Thirty Years' War were signed on October 24, 1648 at Münster in Westphalia (peace with France) and at Osnabrück (peace with Sweden). In addition to the important territorial changes which resulted, the three great confessions of Germany, the Roman Catholic, Lutheran, and Reformed, were accorded equal rights. The Peace underscored the political impotence of the Holy Roman Empire, and opened Germany effectively to continuing foreign influence. The principles upon which it was based dominated international relations in the West until the French Revolution.

32. *Ehrn* is an abbreviated form for "Euer Ehrwürden." It is an obsolete form of address for a Protestant clergyman, corresponding to the Roman Catholic "Hochwürden."

35. *General Pfuhl*. Adam von Pfuhl or Pfuel, Swedish general who lost out in the power struggle following the death of Banér in 1641. Pfuhl had hoped to succeed Banér, who was his brother-in-law, as commander-in-chief of the Swedish forces in Germany. He defected to Denmark, where he became military adviser to King Christian. He died in 1659.

*Page 162*

2–3. *Gallas*. Mathias Gallas (1584–1647), an Austrian general in the imperial service. Gallas proved his worth as a commander by defeating Bernhard of Weimar at Nördlingen and in other campaigns. Though highly regarded by Wallenstein, Gallas helped engineer his overthrow, inheriting both his command and his estates. Dissipation and neglect of duties led Gallas from one military disaster to another, and earned for him the epithet of *Heerverderber*.

3. *schwedischen Trunk*. If a peasant or a burgher refused to give information to his captors, he was thrown on his back and gagged. Liquid manure and filthy water were then poured down his throat.

4. *Linnard Torstenson*. This brilliant Swedish general (1603–1651) began his career as a page of Gustavus Adolphus, later going to Holland to study the art of war. In 1630 he became the commander of Gustavus' field artillery. Captured in an assault on Wallenstein's forces in 1632, he was exchanged the following year. After Banér's death he became supreme commander of the Swedish forces in Germany, and, although confined to his sedan chair by gout, he conducted highly effective campaigns against the imperial forces, taking Leipzig in 1642 and beating Hatzfeld at Jankov in Bohemia in 1645. He retired from command in 1646 for reasons of health, and in the following year was made Count of Ortala by Queen Christina. Torstenson developed a technique of rendering artillery highly mobile, an achievement which not only gave him an advantage over the enemy but enabled him to cover much territory quickly. Raabe's expression "fliegende Scharen" refers to the latter characteristic of his armies.

25. *der rote Hahn*. The expression "red cock" refers to a conflagration caused by arson.

33. *Wittenberg*. Frederick the Wise founded the University of Wittenberg in this city located on the Elbe river in 1502. It has been rightfully called the "cradle of Protestantism," for it was here that Martin Luther taught from 1507 to 1546, developing the doctrines which were to shake Christendom to its very foundations. It was

also here that Luther burned the papal bull on December 10, 1520. Both Luther and his co-Reformer Melanchthon lie buried in Wittenberg. The university was merged with Halle in 1815.

### Page 163

2–3. *wäre . . . längst verlorengegangen, wie das deutsche Volk.* Here we have an example of the cultural symbolism which characterizes the Novelle. The fate of Friedemann Leutenbacher is explicitly equated with that of the German nation in the Thirty Years' War. Cf. also the words: *wie das deutsche Volk gleich ihm mit gefesselten Händen, zerschlagen und blutig, herausgeschleppt sei und niedergeworfen.* (Ibid. 6–8; further, 198:4–6) Else may be taken as the symbol of hope for the German people; Master Conrad as representing the dilemma of the intellectual amid the devastation of war: "Ich bin ein Sohn deines Volkes und wie das Vaterland in Elend," he says to the pastor (167:33–34); the villagers as representing the degradation of the German masses by this most terrible of wars (186:30–32); finally, the old crone Justine may be seen as an embodiment of the foreboding, mysterious forces of life, which are nevertheless friendly to the good, in this case to Else as an embodiment of the good. (188:17–18; 194:23–34) For a discussion of this kind of symbolism, in general see Robert A. Hall, Jr., *Cultural Symbolism in Literature* (Ithaca, N.Y., 1963). In actuality there are three levels of symbolism in the Novelle: (1) the cultural, (2) the natural, and (3) the religious. Raabe has, however, so skillfully woven his symbols into the natural course of events that they by no means obtrude themselves upon the reader.

8–12. *Der Herr hatte gebrüllt. . . .* I have used the English of the Authorized Version as the best equivalent of Luther's text. Cf. the following verses of Jeremiah 25:30–33: ". . . The Lord shall roar from on high, and utter his voice from his holy habitation . . . he shall give a shout as they that tread the grapes, against all the inhabitants of the earth. A noise shall come even to the ends of the earth. . . . And the slain of the Lord shall be at that day from one end of the earth even unto the other end of the earth; they shall not be lamented, neither gathered, nor buried. . . ."

19–24. *Er hat mein Fleisch. . . .* Lamentations 3:4–7. Translation from Authorized Version.

### Page 164

14. *den Tag Sankt Johannis des Täufers.* St. John's Day is June 24th. The religious observance of the season antedates, however, the Christian calendar, having originated in the pagan celebrations of the summer solstice. According to German folk-belief, the whole of nature undergoes a beneficent change at this time as a result of

the return of the life-giving sun. It is the irony of Else's fate that she is attacked by the villagers precisely on this auspicious day. Raabe's choice of this particular day was, therefore, surely not dictated by the fact that it is sometimes regarded in German folklore as a day of misfortune, as some have maintained. See Oppermann, 471. See also Introduction p. 22 above for a discussion of the symbolic role of St. John's Day.

16. *Bannier.* Raabe's spelling of the surname of Johan Banér (1596–1641), the so-called "Swedish lion." Born of an old family of the Swedish nobility, Banér entered the service of Gustavus Adolphus in 1615, thereafter serving in Russia, Livonia, and Poland. In 1630 he campaigned under Gustavus in Germany, taking part in the first battle of Breitenfeld. The battle of Wittstock on October 4, 1636, in which Banér defeated the imperial forces, was a "classic example of masterly leadership" (*Encyclopaedia Britannica*) and made Swedish power supreme in central Germany. Raabe incorrectly gives the date of the battle as September 24. In 1639 Banér defeated the Saxons at Chemnitz and invaded Bohemia. In the winter of 1640–41 he accomplished the unusual feat of breaking camp and, in alliance with the French, marched on Regensburg, where he took the Reichstag by surprise. He was prevented only by the breaking up of the ice on the Danube from taking the city. Banér is generally regarded as the best of Gustavus' generals.

23. *Schwedenzeit.* The period Raabe has in mind is not in actuality the so-called Swedish Period (1630–35) but the Swedish-French Period (1635–1648).

*Page 165*

6. *Tartaren.* The proper spelling of the word is *Tataren.* As in English it is often spelled with two r's, doubtless under the influence of the Latin *Tartarus;* i.e., Hades or its abyss. Historically, the Tatars are descendants of the men of the Golden Horde, mixed racially and linguistically, though chiefly of Turkic or Mongolic origin. In the present context it is the equivalent of gypsies.

28–30. *das schlafende Mägdlein, welches plötzlich ein Strahl der abendlichen Sonne . . . traf.* The symbolism of light and darkness in the Novelle is most striking. Else's radiance is constantly related to the effulgence of bright sunshine, and here we have the first instance of such identification. See pp. 22–25 of the Introduction for a discussion of the light-darkness symbolism in the Novelle. In the passages: 165:28–31; 179:19–20, 29; 180:16–17; 181:25 we find light from without (the so-called "created light" of the theologians) shining on her in a special way; in the passages: 176:3–6; 184:10–15; 192:11–13; 195:28,31 we find the light emanating from within her ("increated" or spiritual light). Natural or created light also parallels Else's radiance: 164:6; 171:7–9; 184:10–15. In some instances darkness and light mixed constitute an ominous sign: 183:7; 184:35. It is clear that Else has the mystic luminosity of the saint. On this point the words of the Eastern Orthodox theologian Saint Gregory Palamas are apropos: "He who shares the divine energy . . . becomes himself in some sort light; he is joined to the Light, and with the Light he sees in full consciousness all that is hidden from those who have not received this grace." Quoted in Mircea Eliade, *Mephistopheles and the Androgyne: Studies in Religious Myth and Symbol*, trans. J. M. Cohen (New York, 1965), p. 63. Palamas's words clearly apply to Raabe's conception of Else. Wilhelm Fehse writes: " 'Else von der Tanne' gehört zu den erschütterndsten Bildern, die Raabe je gemalt hat. Aber er erfüllt auch hier seinen Dichterberuf, Licht aus Schatten zu greifen. Der helle Schein, der von dem Lager der sterbenden Else ausstrahlt, siegt über das Dunkel dieser Tragödie der Weltflucht." *Wilhelm Raabe* (Braunschweig, 1937), p. 231.

*Page 166*
   1. *Marschalk.* Older form of *Marschall* (Eng., "marshal"). The original Old High German *marah* ("horse") was combined with *scalc* ("servant") to designate a groom. The modern German form was influenced by the French version of the word. In the course of time, the term had come to designate the "supervisor of the princely retinue on journeys and campaigns." See Kluge, *Etymologisches Wörterbuch*, s.v.
   21. *dräuend.* Archaic and poetic form of *drohend.*
   30. *durcheinanderworfele auf seiner Tenne.* The images for this time of testing are drawn from the Bible. Thus Isaiah 27:12: "In that day from the river Euphrates to the Brook of Egypt the Lord will thresh out the grain, and you will be gathered one by one, O people of Israel." (Revised Standard Version) Cf. also Hosea 13:3 and Matthew 3:12: "Whose fan is in his hand, and he will thoroughly purge his floor, and gather his wheat into the garner; but he will burn up the chaff with unquenchable fire." Likewise, Luke 3:17.

*Page 167*
   4. *sintemalen.* Archaic for *da* or *weil.*
   20–21. *Mit Wunder.* Archaic for *verwundert.*
   27. *bot . . . die Zeit.* Archaic form for *grüßen.*
   28. *Domine. . . . Non sum impostor*, etc. . . . The fact that Master Conrad speaks in Latin indicates his willingness to accept the pastor while at the same time rejecting the villagers. Thus, the stranger in their midst builds another wall of separation between himself and Leutenbacher's degraded parishioners.

*Page 170*

24–25. *Wittstocker Schlacht.* See note to page 4 under *Bannier.*

*Page 171*

9. *Niederfall des Reiches.* See note to page 1 under *das Römische Reich Deutscher Nation.* Nature is oblivious to the movements of history. Therefore, the cultural symbolism of the Novelle is associated with the characters portrayed.

*Page 173:1—174–27*

*Der Pfarrer hatte . . . immerdar aufs innigste mit der Natur verkehrt* etc. The symbolism of the forest is important in the narrative. Before Else's arrival there, the pastor had quite ambivalent feelings about the woodland: on the one hand it was the only refuge from his depressing surroundings in the village, and consequently he reveled in its mystery, its pleasantness, and its solemnity. The fact that he composed the third part of his sermons in the forest bespeaks his quasi-religious attitude toward it. On the other hand, he often became so frightened and depressed by it that he had to flee from it. In such a way the myth of Pan, who causes *panic* fear in the forest is corroborated in Leutenbacher's experience (though Raabe makes no such classical allusion). All this is because the forest has no soul. Only when Else moves into the forest does it receive a soul, and become altogether pleasant to him. (179:13–22) So closely is Else identified with the forest that in the climactic church-scene the pastor imagines, despite the ominous murmurings of the parishioners, that he is alone with Else in the secure, sunny forest (184:11–15). Therefore, the statement by Johannes Klein that "das Leitmotiv, die hohe Tanne, ist sinnbildlich für den Anhauch großer Natur um Else" is somewhat misleading. (See *Geschichte der deutschen Novelle*, Wiesbaden, 1954, p. 323) In his final delirium, lacerated and stumbling, Friedemann is unconsciously driven to the high ground in the forest from which he and Else had enjoyed the splendid view, and there he collapses and dies. (196:27–31, 197:1–3) Friedemann's forest is a *Tannenwald* and it is with the forest as a whole, not simply the fir tree beneath which she lives, that Else is identified.

7. *die Namen, die Adam den Dingen gegeben.* Cf. Genesis 2:20: "And Adam gave names to all cattle, and to the fowl of the air, and to every beast of the field. . . ."

15. *theatro.* Dative of *theatrum,* which is a Latin borrowing from the Greek.

*Page 174*

19. *Undine.* The name derives from Latin *unda,* meaning "wave." In Fouqué's well-known fairy tale (1811) she is the daughter of a

sea-prince. Being a water spirit, she lacks a human soul. Upon learning that the only way in which she can acquire a soul is through the requited love of a human being, she marries the knight Huldbrand, whose later faithlessness causes her to drown him and herself with tears. There are operas by E. T. A. Hoffmann (1816) and Lortzing (1845), and in recent years Jean Giraudoux has dramatized the tale (1939). It is illuminating to note that Fouqué's Undine, the personification of an element of nature, is also a kind of saint of nature, the purity of whose love is beyond that of ordinary mortals. Because Undine is merely a creature of the imagination, a human being will have to take her place. Else von der Tanne is that human being. See Introduction, esp. pp. 23, 28, 30–31, 39–41.

*Page 175*

1. *jach.* Archaic form of *jäh.*
4. *Hypericum.* The Latin name for St.-John's-wort, which is also used commonly in English. "A large and widely distributed genus of herbs or shrubs (family Guttiferae) that are characterized chiefly by their pentamerous and often showy yellow flowers." *Webster's Third New International Dictionary.* The reference here is probably to *Hypericum perforatum,* known also as *Hartheu, Johannisblut,* and *Hexenkraut.* It was once widely used for medicinal purposes (antihelminthic and purgative) as well as for magical purposes.
4. *sonsten.* Archaic form of *sonst* (Chancery style).

*Page 176*

29. *Domschule.* School associated with a cathedral and designed to educate children of the nobility in the seven liberal arts. The cathedral school in Magdeburg was not founded, however, until 1674. At the time of the destruction of the city there was only one secondary school, later called the *altstädtisches Gymnasium.* See Oppermann, 471.
29. *unglückliche Stadt Magdeburg.* Situated on the Elbe River, Magdeburg has been of strategic economic and military importance since the tenth century. In 1524 it defected to the Reformation, and by the seventeenth century was a firm bulwark of Protestantism. In 1629 it successfully resisted Wallenstein's seven months' siege, but was taken by Tilly on May 20, 1631. To keep the city from falling into the hands of the enemy, it was put to the torch by some of its inhabitants. As a result of the conflagration and the fighting, it is reported that nearly 40,000 inhabitants perished. Only the cathedral, the *Liebfrauenkloster,* and some huts along the Elbe remained standing.
33–34. *die tausend jammervollen Menschen.* Here and in the following

data concerning the conditions at Magdeburg, Raabe relies on F. W. Hoffmann's *Geschichte der Stadt Magdeburg*, III, 1850. Elsewhere he deviates from Hoffmann's account, however, on several scores; e.g., the letter to the cities and villages lying downstream concerning the bodies thrown into the Elbe was actually written, according to Hoffmann, by an individual, not by the survivors of Magdeburg in general; and, further, the number of corpses thus disposed of was put at 6,400 by Hoffmann instead of 6,000. These and other discrepancies suggest that Raabe was citing the facts from memory. See Oppermann, 470–71.

*Page 177*

1. *Tilly*. Johann Tserclaes Graf von Tilly was born in Brabant in 1559, and died in 1632. Educated by Jesuits, he received his training in the Spanish armies, later serving in the imperial army against the Turks. In 1618 he became commander-in-chief of the armies of the Catholic League, and by virtue of a series of victories between 1620 and 1626 he established the superiority of Catholic arms in Germany. In 1630 he succeeded to Wallenstein's post as supreme commander of the imperial armies, capturing Magdeburg in 1631. In the same year he was defeated at Breitenfeld by Gustavus Adolphus, and in the following year was mortally wounded near Ingolstadt. It is unlikely that he actually intended the destruction of that city, since it would have undoubtedly been of strategic importance to him as a base of operations. It is more likely that its devastation was due to the scorched earth policy of its hard-core defenders, who were led by a Swedish commander.

24–25. *Wallonen*. The Walloons of southeast Belgium and northern France are the descendants of the Gauls living in that area at the time of the Roman conquest. Thus they are of Celtic, not Germanic origin. Their language is a dialect of French.

25. *Kroaten*. South Slavic peoples dwelling along the Sava and Drava rivers in southeastern Europe. At the time of the Thirty Years' War, most of their territory was occupied by the Turks, but part of it passed to Austria.

30. *Halberstadt*. A city of Saxony dating from 814, located near the edge of the Harz Forest on the Holzemme River. Else's song about Bishop Buko of Halberstadt (191:15) is a reminder that her father had taken her there before the move into the forest.

*Page 178*

9–24. *Vierzehn lange, lange Wochen*. . . . Else's song is the oldest part of the narrative. According to Raabe's diary, it was written December 13, 1857, and had the title "Verlorene Stadt."

10. *Liga*. The Catholic League was founded on July 10, 1609 under the leadership of Maximilian I of Bavaria to counter the Protestant

Union. It included the archbishoprics of Trier, Mainz, Cologne, and other cities and states of southwest Germany. The leading members of the Protestant Union were the Palatinate, Baden, and Württemberg.

15. *dreißigtausand Ketzerleben.* See note to page 16:33–34.

18–25. *Stadt gewonnen! all gewonnen!* etc. Raabe utilized Friedrich Richter, *Magdeburg, die wieder emporgerichtete Stadt Gottes auf Erden* (Zerbst, 1831), p. 186, where the author writes concerning the destruction of Magdeburg: "Seit Trojas und Jerusalems Zerstörung, berichtete man nach Wien, ist keine größere Viktoria erfahren und erhört worden."

*Page 179*

13–22. *Es war ein ander Ding. . . . .* One might raise the question as to the depth psychological meaning of Else's effect on Friedemann Leutenbacher. No doubt the Freudians in particular would have much to say on this score. More pertinent, however, is another question, namely, in what way does Else affect Friedemann's way of viewing the world? Thus, in what sense does she teach him a way of *knowing?* Raabe supplies the answer in this and other passages. It is clear that Friedemann has always been an intuitive thinker, closely attuned to nature, and utterly unlike the scientific naturalist who sees nature abstractly (Cf. 173:1–26). It may seem that the presence of Else could do little to enhance his normally intuitive perceptions, but Raabe assures us that she does, even to the extent of banishing the panic dread which often overcame him in the forest (17–19). She taught him the language of nature, whether animate or inanimate (19–22). Undoubtedly we have to do with eros here, but it is eros sublimated to the extent that it affects cognition only. A parallel has been drawn between *Else von der Tanne* and Hauptmann's *Der Ketzer von Soana,* a comparison which is indeed justified up to a certain point. The clergymen are in both cases driven to identify with outcast maidens, but eros is expressed quite differently in the two cases: in Hauptmann's story it is expressed in sexual terms, in Raabe's it remains platonic; i.e., it is sublimated. See *Erläuterungen zu Wilhelm Raabe's Else von der Tanne,* Königs Erläuterungen zu den Klassikern, No. 220, 2nd ed. Edgar Neis (Hollfeld/Obfr., n.d.), pp. 27–37.

*Page 180*

21. *Pfingsten. Whitsuntide or Pentecost.* Whitsunday is the fiftieth day after Easter, and celebrates the outpouring of the Holy Spirit upon the apostles according to Acts 2.

8. *Hüfte Jakobs auf der Stätte Pnuel.* See Genesis 32: "And Jacob was left alone; and there wrestled a man with him until the break-

ing of the day. And when he saw that he prevailed not against him, he touched the hollow of his thigh; and the hollow of Jacob's thigh was out of joint, as he wrestled with him. And he said, Let me go, for the day breaketh. And he said, I will not let thee go, except thou bless me . . . And he said, Thy name shall be called no more Jacob, but Israel: for as a prince hast thou power with God and with men, and hast prevailed . . . And he blessed him there. And Jacob called the name of the place Peniel: for I have seen God face to face, and my life is preserved." (Verses 24–26, 28, 29, 30) The author's identification of the scars on Leutenbacher's wrists with the shrunken sinew of Jacob's thigh can only mean that the pastor's suffering had ultimately redemptive meaning. The place Peniel or Penuel (meaning in Hebrew "God's countenance") is located south of the Jabok River, an eastern tributary of the Jordan.

*Page 181*

6. *die letzte Nachtigall.* Oppermann has pointed out that nightingales do not appear in the Harz Forest. He asserts further that this is one of the rare instances when Raabe departs from realism, ascribing this deviation to the desire to associate another romantic symbol with the roe and the moonlight. (472)

10–11. *Die ganze Nacht hindurch war er von bösen, angstvollen Träumen geplagt.* Although the subconscious disturbances indicated by such dreams did not enter into Friedemann's consciousness to the extent of affecting his decision to receive Else at the church, they do, nevertheless, betray a real ambivalence in his attitude. However, his external behavior betrays no such ambivalence: all his actions were directed to the one end of joyfully receiving Else at the service and of administering the sacraments to her. Even when Else and Master Conrad arrived and were clearly in danger from the aroused parishioners, the pastor failed to respond as one would normally expect. The ecstasy induced by Else's visit to the church rendered him insensitive to the impending danger. If Leutenbacher is regarded as the real protagonist of the tale (as, from some standpoints, he certainly may be), one might say that his error is to be equated with the hamartia of the tragic hero.

*Page 182*

7. *fürder—.* Archaic and poetic for *weiter.*

24. *fürbaß.* Archaic and poetic form for *fort und fort* or *weiter.*

*Page 183*

*Herzeleins pochend Weben.* . . . These lines are from Raabe's poem "Sonnenschein" of October 24, 1861.

*Page 184*

19. *drei Hände voll Erde.* Earth from a grave was widely believed to be effective against the spell of a witch. Oppermann, 472.

23. *Hatzfeld.* Melchior von Hatzfeldt (1593–1658), a general in the service of the imperial forces in the Thirty Years' War, took part in the conspiracy against Wallenstein, and was handsomely rewarded with a large estate in Silesia. Hatzfeldt fought successfully in the Rhine-Westphalian campaigns, but was defeated badly by the Swedes at Wittstock (1636) and at Jankov (1645), being captured in the latter battle. After retirement he returned to the service of the German emperor, helping to rescue Poland from the Swedes in 1657.

24. *aufhängten.* According to German folk-belief everything associated with an executed person brings good luck and is effective against witchcraft. Oppermann, 472.

*Page 185*

2. *Kobolden.* In German folklore these earth- or house-imps are dwarf-like and ugly, but may be either helpful or harmful. In Raabe's use they are obviously of the latter type.

10. *das schlechte Zinngefäß.* The word "schlecht" is used here in the sense of "schlicht," a meaning which it retains in the expression "schlecht und recht." Hence, the meaning "simple" or "modest."

*Page 186*

10–11. *Sie weichen nicht; lasset uns gehen; sie werden nicht wagen uns anzufallen.* Although highly idealistic, Master Conrad was never a man of faith. (He is a good example of the type Nietzsche called "Alexandrian" or "Socratic" man: he even reads Plato as Else lies dying. 194:28) It is therefore characteristic that in this perilous situation he *reasons* that the parishioners will not dare to harm him or Else. Else, on the other hand, reveals her deep religious faith with the words: "Gott wird uns schützen, jetzt wie immer; ja lasset uns gehen." Thus both father and daughter make the same decision, but from very different standpoints. As for Friedemann, he is only jolted out of his ecstatic trance by the now obviously murderous intentions of the villagers; as a consequence he is seized by a fearful anxiety, and can only hope that his priestly authority will somehow function as a shield against the superstitious mob.

*Page 188*

23. *"Er hat mich in Finsternis gelegt. . . ."* Lamentations 3:6. Cf. 163:22 and 196:24. The threefold repetition of this Biblical passage at dramatic points in the narrative is highly significant for the light-darkness symbolism of the Novelle: it confirms Leutenbacher's belief in the ultimate victory of darkness over light as far

as this earthly existence is concerned. See further the following passages where darkness is related to Else's death: 164:2–3; 179:1–4; 182:33; 183:7; to his own death: 196:11–13 and the passage cited above; to Conrad's death: 197:35–198–1; to cosmic darkness and chaos: 180:13–14; 195:27–28. See the Introduction, pp. 22–25, for a discussion of the light-darkness symbolism.

## Page 191

15. *Buko.* Usually identified with Burchard II, Bishop of Halberstadt (1059–1088), who lives in legend as a friend of children, but whom history depicts only as an ambitious and warlike ecclesiastic.

15–16. *Kinderlied vom guten Bischof Buko von Halberstadt.* A Low German version of the folksong begins: "Buhköken von Halberstadt, bring doch unse Lieschen wat!" The following High German version appears in *Des Knabes Wunderhorn,* Vollständige Ausgabe, (Munich, n.d.), p. 6:

> Buko von Halberstadt,
> Bring doch meinem Kinde was.
> Was soll ich ihm bringen?
> Rote Schuh mit Ringen,
> Schöne Schuh mit Gold beschlagen,
> Die soll unser Kindchen tragen.

> Hurraso, Burra fort,
> Wagen und schöne Schuh sind fort,
> Stecken tief im Sumpfe,
> Pferde sind ertrunken,
> Hurra, schrei nicht, Reitersknecht,
> Warum fährst du auch so schlecht!

21. *Königsmark.* Hans Christoph, Graf von Königsmark (1600–63) was born in Brandenburg and began his military career in the imperial army. When Gustavus Adolphus appeared in Germany in 1630 however, he defected to the Protestant side, ultimately becoming a field-marshal in the Swedish army. From his base in Westphalia he roamed freely through much of Germany, taking much booty and causing great devastation. Upon returning to Sweden he was enfeoffed by Queen Christina and granted the hereditary title of count.

## Page 194

28. *Platonis hohes Buch Phädon.* Plato's *Phaedo* deals with the death of Socrates and the question of the immortality of the soul. It is significant that Master Conrad, as a true intellectual, turns to philosophy rather than religion in his hour of distress.

*Page 195*

13–30. *Jawohl, wehe uns! Es ist geschehen,* etc. Fritz Lockemann calls *Else von der Tanne* a "Gegennovelle," because the "powers of chaos" achieve an absolute victory over order in the world. *Gestalt und Wandlungen der deutschen Novelle* (München, 1957), p. 242. Whether his distinctions are basic to the interpretation of the Novelle in general or not, it cannot be denied that *Else* fits this category. The present declaration of the victory of chaos over order by Friedemann Leutenbacher could scarcely be more unambiguous. The language of this peroration is almost a Biblical cento. See Appendix A for a listing of the Biblical phrases and allusions present in Leutenbacher's language.

22. *fürder.* See note to page 22:7.

26. *der Antichrist.* Cf. II John 7.

*Page 196*

24. "Er hat mich in Finsternis gelegt . . ." Cf. 163:22 and 188:23 and note to latter.

*Page 198*

5–6. *diesen deutschen Krieg, welcher dreißig Jahre gedauert hat.* Wilhelm Fehse says of Raabe's historical Novelle: " 'Else von der Tanne' ist die erschütterndste Darstellung der Not der Dreißigjährigen Krieges, die wir in unserem Schrifttum besitzen. Das Grauen einer entarteten Kriegsführung mag von anderen vielleicht noch furchtbarer geschildert worden sein; aber Raabe dringt über dieses Grauen noch hinaus zu der hoffnungslosen seelischen Verwüstung vor, die diese gnadenloseste Zeit der deutschen Geschichte heraufführte." *Wilhelm Raabe,* p. 229.

# Appendix A

## BIBLICAL QUOTATIONS AND ALLUSIONS
## IN *ELSE VON DER TANNE*

(Generally after Oppermann. Principal references are in capital letters.
Figures in square brackets refer to German text.)

### OLD TESTAMENT

| | |
|---|---|
| GENESIS 32:24–30 | [180:7] |
| Genesis 2:20 | [173:7] |
| I Chronicles 28:20 | [195:14] |
| Ezra 10:2 | [195:15] |
| Job 15:25 | [195:17] |
| Psalm 37:13 | [195:21] |
| Psalm 94:14 | [195:14–15] |
| Isaiah 27:12 | [166:29] |
| Isaiah 14:27 | [195:22] |
| JEREMIAH 25:30–33 | [163:8–12] |
| LAMENTATIONS 3:4–7 | [163:19–24] |

### NEW TESTAMENT

| | |
|---|---|
| Matthew 3:12 | [166:30] |
| Matthew 5:13 | [195:22–23] |
| Matthew 6:13 | [195:30] |
| Matthew 16:18 | [195:29] |
| Luke 22:20 | [185:6] |
| Luke 23:34 | [194:17] |
| I Corinthians 11:24 | [185:6] |
| II Thessalonians 5:2 | [195:18] |
| John: 7 | [180:16] |

# *Appendix B*

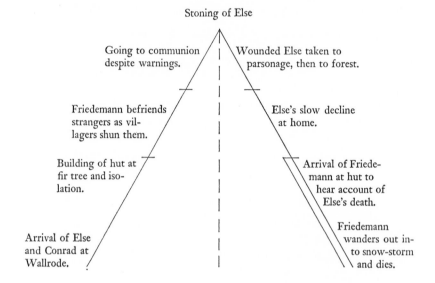

Stoning of Else

Going to communion despite warnings.

Wounded Else taken to parsonage, then to forest.

Friedemann befriends strangers as villagers shun them.

Else's slow decline at home.

Building of hut at fir tree and isolation.

Arrival of Friedemann at hut to hear account of Else's death.

Arrival of Else and Conrad at Wallrode.

Friedemann wanders out into snow-storm and dies.

Double line on lower right of diagram represents coinciding of frame narrative and flashback (*Binnenhandlung*). Broken line from apex to base of pyramid divides it into two halves, illustrating bilateral aspect of this type of analysis.

# SELECTED BIBLIOGRAPHY

Dose, Helene. 1928. *Die Magie bei Wilhelm Raabe*. Berlin: Klemm.

Ehrentreich, Alfred. 1949. *"Else von der Tanne*—ein Flüchtlings-schicksal." *Die neue Schau* 10:300–301.

Fairley, Barker. 1960. *Wilhelm Raabe: An Introduction to His Novels*. London: Oxford University Press.

Fehse, Wilhelm. 1928. *Wilhelm Raabes Leben*. Berlin: Klemm.

———. 1940. *In alls gedultig—Briefe Wilhelm Raabes*. Berlin: Grote.

Hanson, William P. 1968. "Some Basic Themes in Raabe." *German Life and Letters* 21:122–130.

Helmers, Hermann, ed. 1968. *Raabe in neuer Sicht*. Berlin: Kohlhammer.

———. 1968. *Wilhelm Raabe*. Stuttgart: Metzler.

Hoppe, Karl. 1962–. *Wilhelm Raabe: Sämtliche Werke*. Göttingen: Vandenhoeck und Ruprecht.

———. 1967. *Wilhelm Raabe: Beiträge zum Verständnis seiner Person und seines Werkes*. Göttingen: Vandenhoeck und Ruprecht.

Killy, Walther. 1963. "Das Odfeld," in *Wirklichkeit und Kunstcharakter*. Pp. 146–165. Reprinted in Helmers 1968.

King, Janet K. 1967. "Raabe's Else von der Tanne." 1967. *The German Quarterly* 40:653–663.

Lukács, Georg. 1964. "Wilhelm Raabe," in *Deutsche Literatur in zwei Jahrhunderten*. Berlin: Luchterhand. Pp. 420–451. Reprinted in Helmers 1968.

Maatje, Frank C. 1961. "Ein früher Ansatz zur 'stream of consciousness'—Dichtung. Raabes 'Altershausen'." *Neophilologus* 45:305–323.

Martini, Fritz. 1935. "Das Formgesetz der Dichtung Wilhelm Raabes." *Mitteilungen für die Gesellschaft der Freunde Wilhelm Raabes* 25:91–107.

———. 1960. "Forschungsbericht zur deutschen Literatur in der Zeit des Realismus." *Deutsche Vierteljahrsschrift für Literaturwissenschaft und Geistesgeschichte* 34:640–650.

———. 1964. *Deutsche Literatur im bürgerlichen Realismus*. Stuttgart: Metzler. Pp. 665–736.

Mayer, Gerhart. 1960. *Die geistige Entwicklung Wilhelm Raabes.* Göttingen: Vandenhoeck und Ruprecht.

Meyer, Hermann. 1953. "Raum und Zeit in Wilhelm Raabes Erzählkunst." *Deutsche Vierteljahrsschrift für Literaturwissenschaft und Geistesgeschichte* 27:236–267. Reprinted in Helmers 1968.

———. 1961. *Das Zitat in der Erzählkunst.* Stuttgart: Metzler. Pp. 186–206.

———. 1963. *Der Sonderling in der deutschen Dichtung.* Munich: Hanser. Pp. 229–289.

*Mitteilungen für die Gesellschaft der Freunde Wilhelm Raabes.* 1911–. Wolfenbüttel: Heckner.

Ohl, Hubert. 1968. *Bild und Wirklichkeit.* Heidelberg: Stiehm.

Oppermann, Hans. 1964. "Zum Problem der Zeit bei Wilhelm Raabe." *Raabe-Jahrbuch* n.v.: 57–77. Reprinted in Helmers 1969.

Pascal, Roy. 1954. "The Reminiscence-Technique in Raabe." *The Modern Language Review* 49:339–348. Reprinted in German translation in Helmers 1968.

Pongs, Hermann. 1958. *Wilhelm Raabe: Leben und Werk.* Heidelberg: Quelle und Meyer.

*Raabe-Gedenkbuch.* 1921. Berlin: Klemm.

Radcliffe, Stanley. 1969. "Wilhelm Raabe, The Thirty Years War, and the Novelle." *German Life and Letters* 220–229.

von Wiese, Benno. 1962. *Die deutsche Novelle von Goethe bis Kafka.* Vol. 2, pp. 198–215.

# Index